Mathew McDermott is a barrister in London. He specialises in property law with a particular focus on the law relevant to landlords and tenants (residential and commercial).

A Practical Guide to Rent Repayment Orders

A Practical Guide to Rent Repayment Orders

Mathew McDermott

Barrister

42BR Barristers, London

Law Brief Publishing

Published 2025 by Law Brief Publishing, an imprint of Law Brief Publishing Ltd
30 The Parks
Minehead
Somerset
TA24 8BT

www.lawbriefpublishing.com

Paperback: 978-1-916698-70-3

PREFACE

The making of rent repayment orders ("RROs") against residential landlords in England has risen over the last few years, a rise brought about by the coming into force of Part 2, Chapter 4 of the Housing and Planning Act 2016. Now in England the First-tier Tribunal (Property Chamber) is frequently considering applications -- usually by tenants -- seeking an order that would see their landlord have to 'repay' some of the rent that had been received. To get to that stage, however, the Tribunal will first have to be satisfied that the landlord has committed a particular housing-related offence.

This is why RROs are one tool -- part of a larger set of tools – aimed at improving standards in the private rented lettings market and rooting out landlords who do not comply.

Furthermore, the increase in the making of RROs shall continue as a result changes to the RRO scheme to be brought about by Sir Kier Starmer's Labour Government in the form of its Renters' Rights Bill, which at the time of writing is going through Parliament. The scope of the RRO regime will be broadened and the maximum amount increased – with what some might call 'loopholes' being closed down, alongside other changes.

This book will therefore assist any practitioner working in this growing area of landlord and tenant litigation. It will assist anyone requiring an understanding of the substantive law – what are they, when will they be made, how are they quantified – as well as the practical procedural steps relating to the bringing of and responding to applications for RROs and challenging any orders made – when, where and how.

The law is believed to be correct as of 1st December 2024. The book applies only to England.

Mathew McDermott
December 2024

CONTENTS

CHAPTER ONE

AN INTRODUCTION TO RENT REPAYMENT ORDERS IN ENGLAND

A rent repayment order ("RRO") as discussed in this book is essentially what the name suggests it would be: an order usually requiring rent to be repaid by a landlord usually to their tenant or tenants.

In simple terms, if the landlord is said to have committed a particular prescribed offence then it may be open to their tenant to seek an order requiring them to repay an amount contained in the order.

A similar procedure exists for the benefit of local housing authorities ("LHA") where universal credit or housing benefit has been paid.

The regime relating to these RROs in England on which this book focuses is to be found in Chapter 4 within Part 2 of the Housing and Planning Act 2016 ("the HPA 2016").

Chapter 4 currently contains only twelve sections that comprise its RRO framework, and it is illuminating in terms of identifying the purpose of an RRO to note the title of Part 2 within which this framework is found: "*Rogue Landlords and Property Agents in England*". The scheme acts to ensure housing standards are complied with or, where they are not, to drive out from the sector those rogue landlords.

These twelve sections comprise the main framework for RROs in England on which this book focuses. They explain, amongst other things, the meaning of an RRO, who can get them, time limits in respect of applying for one, who may be subject to them, when they are available, how to work out the amount of them and where to bring an application for one – amongst other matters.

The purpose of this book is to explain how this regime applies in England.

A broader reach

As will be shown, there has in recent years been a rise in tenants seeking RROs against their landlord.

This rise is primarily due to the fact that the rent repayment order regime as contained in the Housing Act 2004 was in comparison to the regime on which this book focuses – the 12 provisions contained in Chapter 4 of Part 2 of the HPA 2016 – narrower in its scope and application.

Chapter 4 of Part 2 of the HPA 2016, however, introduced a regime relating to RROs that was in its scope much broader – and in significant ways.

Furthermore the breadth of this RRO regime will continue to grow. This is because of a number of proposed changes relating to it contained in the Renters' Rights Bill 2024–25. The Bill was introduced to the House of Commons on 11th September 2024 by Sir Kier Starmer's Labour government. It received its second reading on 9th October 2024 and, at the time of writing, has just completed Committee Stage.

Because of the size of the current Government's majority in the House of Commons it is highly likely that the Bill will pass and probably in the form discussed in this book, although as at the time of writing it is still possible that provisions will change, so the precise wording of the final changes is not known for certain.

What follows is a brief summary of this legislative development. What it shows, however, is a point that is central to the regime itself, namely that

RROs exist to try to force landlords in the private rented sector to comply with the law and, in particular, to meet certain housing standards. Those that do not comply will be penalised – and may be forced out of the market altogether.

RROs are one tool to be used to reach these ends.

The Rent Repayment Order regime as contained in the Housing Act 2004

As referred to above the making of a 'Rent Repayment Order' – the power to order a landlord to repay to their tenant certain sums of money in certain prescribed situations – was not created by Chapter 4 in Part 2 of the HPA 2016.

The Housing Act 2004 gave a right to LHAs or occupiers to apply to the First-tier Tribunal (Property Chamber) ("the FTT") to seek an order that certain sums paid by them during a particular period be repaid.

The general framework within the relevant parts of the Housing Act 2004 could broadly be summarised as permitting applications to the FTT in the following circumstances:

- Applications made by an LHA or an occupier (a tenant or licensee) seeking an order requiring repayment of money paid usually to the landlord – most typically, but not necessarily, this would be rent or, in the case of the housing authority, housing benefit or universal credit;

- The payments in question would had to have been made during a particular period of time that related to when a particular offence had been committed;

- In this respect, it might have been alleged that the landlord had committed an offence concerning a failure to obtain a particular licence relating to the occupation of the property in circumstances where the law required there to be one; and

- There was a 12-month time limit or 'limitation period' in which such applications to the FTT would have to be made that was linked to the occurrence of a particular event. This ultimately depended upon the nature of the application in question (one such event, for example, was the date of the conviction for the applicable licensing offence).

As shown in this book much of this framework is generally speaking contained within the RRO regime in the HPA 2016.

There exists, however, key differences between the regime in the Housing Act 2004 and the regime dealt with in this book that is contained in Chapter 4 of Part 2 of the HPA 2016:

- **The offences**: under the Housing Act 2004, an application for an RRO could only be made in relation to certain 'licensing offences': in simple terms, where a landlord was required by law to have a particular licence relating to particular occupied property, but did not have such a licence. As stated below, the regime in the HPA 2016 expands the list of offences beyond those relating just to licensing;

- **Need for a conviction**: if a tenant wanted to make an application to the FTT for an RRO under the Housing Act 2004 they had to satisfy the FTT that the landlord had been convicted of one of the applicable licensing offences or that the LHA had received an RRO itself in relation to housing benefit or universal credit;

- **Tenants not empowered**: the natural consequence of the above was that in reality the tenant had minimal power of their own, as their application would be dependent upon others to have already taken certain steps successfully in respect of their landlord e.g obtaining a conviction.

The RRO regime in Chapter 4 of Part 2 of the Housing and Planning Act 2016

From 6th April 2017 by virtue of Part 2 of the HPA 2016 the regime for RROs in England was expanded. As referred to above, this was part of a desire to deter "*Rogue Landlords and Property Agents in England*".

In contrast with the regime in the Housing Act 2004 before it, an application for an RRO could now be made by a tenant or an LHA to the FTT against a person who was alleged to have committed one of seven listed offences:

1) violence for securing entry;
2) eviction or harassment of occupiers;
3) failure to comply with improvement notice;
4) failure to comply with prohibition order, etc;
5) control or management of unlicensed HMO;
6) control or management of unlicensed house; and
7) breach of a banning order.

Section 40 (1) & (2) of the HPA 2016 is central to the RRO regime in the HPA 2016:

> *"(1) This Chapter confers power on the First-tier Tribunal to make a rent repayment order where a landlord has committed an offence to which this Chapter applies.*

> *(2) A rent repayment order is an order requiring the landlord under a tenancy of housing in England to—*
>
> *(a) repay an amount of rent paid by a tenant, or*
>
> *(b) pay a local housing authority an amount in respect of a relevant award of universal credit paid (to any person) in respect of rent under the tenancy..."*

The 'offence' in question is not now one in respect of which the landlord must be 'convicted'. The FTT must instead be satisfied beyond reasonable doubt that the landlord has 'committed' the offence. Furthermore, although the licensing offences relating to the RRO regime within the Housing Act 2004 remain as the list above shows there has been added five additional offences relating to a wider range of dealings than just the licensing of particular property.

In Chapter 2 these offences – which effectively act as a gateway for the making of an application for an RRO – are addressed in detail.

Another change brought about by the introduction of the RRO regime within the HPA 2016 relates to the approach taken by the FTT in determining the amount that shall be payable under an RRO. This approach to quantification of the orders is the subject of Chapter 4.

Likely changes to the RRO regime in the Housing and Planning Act 2016 by the Renters' Rights Bill 2024-25

On 11th September 2024 Sir Kier Starmer's Labour government published the Renters' Rights Bill.

At the time of writing the Bill had received its second reading in the House of Commons and had just completed the committee stage.

As a result, it is impossible to know yet in exactly what terms the RRO regime in the HPA 2016 will be changed. That it will be changed and will be changed substantially, however, is something about which one can be almost certain – this following from the substantial majority that the government currently enjoys in the House of Commons.

The approach taken in this book to the relevant changes to the RRO regime in the HPA 2016 proposed by this Bill is to discuss each proposal as it applies to the current law. In other words, rather than list these proposed changes likely to be brought about by the Renters' Rights Bill in a standalone chapter, this book instead discusses each proposal in its proper context at the end of each chapter, such as in Chapter 2 in respect of the grounds that permit an application for an RRO and how those grounds are to be expanded, and in Chapter 4 in relation to how the approach to the assessment of the amount of the RRO is likely to change.

What is clear, however, is that the general direction in which the RRO regime has been going is continuing: the scope and application of RROs is likely to widen further as successive governments see them as one way of deterring rogue landlords and enforcing compliance with important housing laws and standards.

The Ministry of Housing, Communities & Local Government has published its "*Guide to the Renters' Rights Bill*" (updated 26th September 2024). As this guidance says in respect of the Government's wishes for the RRO regime in the HPA 2016 in England:

> *"We are introducing a package of measures to strengthen rent repayment orders. The measures will increase the deterrent effect of rent repayment orders, make them easier and more appealing for tenants and local authorities to pursue and expand them to cover more of the sector".*

Although it is possible that the Bill may change in relation to RROs, what is almost certain is that the growth seen in recent years in applications for RROs to the FTT is likely to continue. The proposals in the Bill as currently drafted include, for example, the doubling of the maximum amount of rent a landlord can be ordered to pay, further adding to the number of offences that would allow an application for an RRO to be made and extending their reach further by permitting applications to be brought against superior landlords and company directors.

Summary

- This book deals with RROs in England, namely the provisions in Chapter 4 of Part 2 of the Housing and Planning Act 2016;

- The following chapters deal with key questions that any practitioner working in this area of law is likely to need to know the answer to: what are RROs under the HPA 2016? In what circumstances can one be sought and awarded? To and against whom? How much is one likely to be? What is the procedure for making, defending and thereafter challenging RROs?

- The scope of these orders has increased since the Housing Act 2004, particularly in respect of the offences or 'gateways through which' an application for an RRO may be made and because of the removal of a requirement that the landlord be convicted of a particular offence;

- Moreover, via proposals in the Renters' Rights Bill extensive and important amendments are expected to the RRO regime in the HPA 2016, and these will be discussed throughout the chapters that follow;

- Considering the size of the current Labour government's parliamentary majority, it is very likely that the proposals within the Renters' Rights Bill will become law and, therefore, that the increase in the number of applications for RROs is likely to continue.

CHAPTER TWO

GROUNDS FOR SEEKING A RENT REPAYMENT ORDER IN ENGLAND UNDER THE HOUSING & PLANNING ACT 2016

Introduction

The aim of this chapter is to answer the following question: in what circumstances might an application for an RRO be made?

The first part of this chapter begins by explaining the meaning of the orders themselves – a 'rent repayment order' – so as to put what follows into context.

The main part of this chapter, however, focuses on the 'offences' – currently, there are seven – which, when committed by a landlord, may entitle a tenant to make an application to the First-tier Tribunal (Property Chamber) ("the FTT") for an RRO.

The chapter covers the essential elements of each of the seven offences. There is a particular emphasis on the two licensing offences contained in sections 72 (1) and 95 (1) of the Housing Act 2004 ("the 2004 Act") as these tend to be the two offences that frequently form the basis of an application to the FTT for an RRO. Practitioners should, however, consider consulting specialist texts applicable to each offence because the level of analysis offered by such texts is beyond the scope of this book.

Finally, the chapter ends by looking ahead to the proposals contained in the Renters' Rights Bill, which at the time of writing has recently completed the committee stage in the House of Commons. The Bill is likely to add to the grounds – to the number of 'offences' – that are discussed in this chapter and make other significant changes to the RRO regime that is in Chapter 4 of Part 2 of the Housing and Planning 2016 ("the HPA 2016").

What is a Rent Repayment Order under Chapter 4 of Part 2 of the Housing and Planning Act 2016?

Put simply – as the name suggests – a rent repayment order ("an RRO") is an order requiring a landlord to repay money (usually but not always rent). To whom the money is to be ordered to be repaid will depend upon who is applying for the order, a tenant or a local housing authority ("an LHA"). By s. 41 of the HPA 2016 applications for an RRO can be made by tenants or by LHAs, but RROs made pursuant to an application by an LHA will be in respect of universal credit paid (to any person) and the LHA must also take an additional step before applying for an RRO in that they must first give a notice of intended proceedings to the landlord explaining that they intend to apply for an RRO and why. This procedure is addressed in more detail in Chapter 5.

As for the meaning of an RRO s.56 (1) of the HPA 2016 states that references within Chapter 4 of Part 2 to a 'rent repayment order' have the meaning given to them by s.40. Section 40 is entitled *"Introduction and key definitions"* and at s.40 (1) and (2) it is stated:

> *"(1) This Chapter confers power on the First-tier Tribunal to make a rent repayment order where a landlord has committed an offence to which this Chapter applies.*
>
> *(2) A rent repayment order is an order requiring the landlord under a tenancy of housing in England to—*
>
> *(a) repay an amount of rent paid by a tenant, or*

> *(b) pay a local housing authority an amount in respect of a relevant award of universal credit paid (to any person) in respect of rent under the tenancy..."*

There is an important time limit relating to when applications for RROs can be made by tenants (see s. 41 (2) (b) of the HPA 2016) in that a tenant can only apply for an RRO if the 'offence' by the landlord that is relied upon was committed in the period of 12 months ending with the day on which the application to the FTT is made.

See Chapter 5 in this respect and in respect of other procedural issues relevant to RRO proceedings.

Currently, the paying party – that is, the party against whom the RRO is made – can only be the immediate landlord of the tenant (see *Rakusen v. Jepsen* [2023] UKSC 9), although the Renters' Rights Bill is likely to change this. The Supreme Court decision of *Rakusen* is discussed in detail in Chapter 3

As stated above, in England the FTT has power to make an RRO where a landlord has committed an offence to which Chapter 4 of Part 2 the HPA 2016 applies (s.40 (1) HPA 2016).

This reference to 'an offence' is a reference to the seven offences contained in a table in s.40 (3) of the HPA 2016 and, subject to other criteria, the FTT will have power to make an RRO where a landlord has committed one of the offences on that list.

Section 40 (3) of the HPA 2016, including the table, is as follows:

> "(3) *A reference to* "an offence to which this Chapter applies" *is to an offence, of a description specified in the table, that is committed by a landlord in relation to housing in England let by that landlord.*

	Act	*section*	*general description of offence*
1	Criminal Law Act 1977	section 6(1)	violence for securing entry
2	Protection from Eviction Act 1977	section 1(2), (3) or (3A)	eviction or harassment of occupiers
3	Housing Act 2004	section 30(1)	failure to comply with improvement notice
4		section 32(1)	failure to comply with prohibition order etc
5		section 72(1)	control or management of unlicensed HMO
6		section 95(1)	control or management of unlicensed house
7	This Act	section 21	breach of banning order

Although s.40 (3) refers to a landlord having 'committed' one of these offences, this does not mean that the landlord must have been 'convicted' of the offence in a criminal court. In this respect s.43 (1) of the HPA 2016 says:

> *"The First-tier Tribunal may make a rent repayment order if satisfied, beyond reasonable doubt, that a landlord has committed an offence to which this Chapter applies (whether or not the landlord has been convicted)."*

This means that the criminal standard of proof applies: the FTT must be satisfied beyond reasonable doubt that a landlord has committed the offence – and not merely that on balance the landlord has.

A further point to note before moving on is that the offence forming the basis of the RRO application must have been committed by a landlord in relation to housing in England let by that landlord. For these purposes references to 'letting' and to 'let' include the grant of a licence, and similarly references to 'tenancy' include a licence (see s.56 of the HPA 2016).

'Housing' in England for these purposes means a building, or part of a building, occupied or intended to be occupied as a dwelling or as more than one dwelling (s. 56 of the HPA 2016).

The Grounds: the Seven Offences in s.40 (3) of the HPA 2016

The first offence included in the table above is contained in s.6 of the Criminal Law Act 1977 ("the CLA 1977").

(1) Violence for securing entry

Subject to certain exceptions, any person who without lawful authority uses or threatens violence for the purpose of securing entry into any premises for himself or for any other person is guilty of an offence, provided that:

(a) there is someone present on those premises at the time who is opposed to the entry which the violence is intended to secure; and

(b) the person using or threatening the violence knows that that is the case.

See s.6 (1) of the CLA 1977.

By s. 6 (1A) of the CLA 1977 this does not apply to a person who is a "displaced residential occupier" or a "protected intending occupier" of the premises in question or who is acting on behalf of such an occupier. These are concepts described in sections 12 and 12A of the CLA 1977, but are unlikely to be of relevance to applications for RROs under the HPA 2016 simply because, as stated, for the FTT to have jurisdiction to make an RRO the offence has to be committed by a landlord in relation to housing in England let by that landlord.

By s. 6 (2) of the CLA 1977 any interest in or right to possession or occupation of the premises that a person has does not constitute 'lawful authority' for the purposes of the s.6 (1) offence. The 'lawful authority' proviso exists for the benefit of people or officers who may have been given authority to enter residential premises, such as County Court bailiffs acting under a Court warrant (as an example).

As to what is meant by using or threatening "violence" for the purpose of securing entry, the CLA 1977 provides no definition but it is immaterial whether the violence is directed against the person or against property and whether the entry which the violence is intended to secure is for the purpose of acquiring possession of the premises in question or for any other purpose (s. 6 (4) of the CLA 1977). What is crucial for the purposes of obtaining an RRO is that the applicant shall need to prove (beyond reasonable doubt) that the use of or the threats of violence were for the purpose of securing entry into any premises.

By s. 12 (1) (a) of the CLA 1977 the reference in s. 6 (1) to 'premises' is broad and means any building, any part of a building under separate occupation, any land ancillary to a building, the site comprising any building or buildings together with any land ancillary thereto.

Although this is a broad definition, once again it needs to be borne in mind that for the purposes of applications for RROs the FTT when considering making an order pursuant to s. 40 (1) of the HPA 2016 is only empowered to do so against a landlord under a tenancy of housing in England. And, as stated above, 'housing' for these purposes means a building, or part of a building, occupied or intended to be occupied as a dwelling or as more than one dwelling.

(2) *Eviction or harassment of occupiers*

The second offence included in the table in s. 40 (3) of the HPA 2016 relates to unlawfully evicting or harassing residential occupiers. There are three separate but similar offences referred to in s. 40 (3).

These offences are contained in s. 1 of the Protection from Eviction Act 1977:

(1) Unlawfully depriving (or attempting to unlawfully deprive) any residential occupier of premises or part of premises of their occupation. There will be no offence where the person proves that they believed, and had reasonable cause to believe, that the residential occupier had ceased to reside in the premises (s. 1 (2) of the Protection from Eviction Act 1977);

(2) where any person with intent to cause the residential occupier of any premises (a) to give up the occupation of the premises or any part of them or (b) to refrain from exercising any right or pursuing any remedy in respect of the premises or part of them does acts likely to interfere with the peace or comfort of the residential occupier or members of their household, or persistently withdraws or withholds services reasonably required for the occupation of the premises as a residence (s.1 (3) of the Protection from Eviction Act 1977); or

(3) where the landlord of a residential occupier or an agent of the landlord (a) does acts likely to interfere with the peace or comfort of the residential occupier or members of their household or (b) persistently withdraws or withholds services reasonably required for the occupation of the premises in question as a residence; and in either case knows, or has reasonable cause to believe, that that conduct is likely to cause the residential occupier to give up the occupation of the whole or part of the premises or to refrain from exercising any right or pursuing any remedy in respect of the whole or part of the premises (s. 1 (3A)

of the Protection from Eviction Act 1977). However, such a person shall not be guilty of this offence if they had reasonable grounds for doing the acts or withdrawing or withholding the services in question (see s. 1 (3A) & (3B) of the Protection from Eviction Act 1977).

See also s.1 (1) of the Protection from Eviction Act 1977 for the meaning of 'residential occupier'.

(3) *Failure to comply with an improvement notice*

The third offence in s. 40 (3) of the HPA 2016 is contained in s.30 (1) of the 2004 Act and relates to a failure to comply with an improvement notice.

In short, s.30 (1) of the 2004 Act makes it an offence for a person on whom an operative improvement notice has been served to fail to comply with it. However, by s.30 (4) it is a defence if that person had a reasonable excuse for failing to comply with it (as where, for example, the landlord was not aware of the content of the notice until the period for complying had passed: see, e.g, *Tabassam v Manchester City Council* [2024] UKUT 93 (LC)).

In contrast to the elements of the offence, it is for the landlord to prove the defence on the balance of probabilities.

An improvement notice is a notice served in respect of residential premises by an LHA requiring the person on whom it is served to take certain specified remedial action in respect of certain specified hazards (s.11 (2) & s.12 (2) of the 2004 Act). The time for beginning and completing the remedial action specified in the notice will differ depending on whether or not an appeal is brought against the notice (see s. 30 (2) of 2004 Act).

The offence in s. 30 (1) of the 2004 Act relates only to an improvement notice that is 'operative'. This is dealt with in s. 15 (1) and (2): an improvement notice becomes operative at the end of the period of 21 days beginning with the day on which it is served, but there are exceptions to this which can be found at s. 15 (3) of the 2004 Act.

The failure to comply is limited to cases where the improvement notice was given in respect of a hazard on the premises let by the landlord (as opposed, for example, to common parts) (s. 40 (4) of the HPA 2016).

(4) Failure to comply with prohibition order, etc

The fourth offence in s. 40 (3) of the HPA 2016 is also contained in the 2004 Act. Section 32 (1) makes it an offence to fail to comply with a 'prohibition order'.

Specifically, it makes it an offence for a person, knowing that a prohibition order has become operative in relation to any specified premises, to use the premises in contravention of that order or to permit the premises to be so used.

It is a defence that the person had a reasonable excuse for using the premises or permitting them to be used in contravention of the prohibition order (s.32 (3) of the 2004 Act).

Prohibition orders are, as the name suggests, orders prohibiting the use of residential premises. An LHA has a power to make a prohibition order where they are satisfied that a category 1 hazard (s.20 (1) of the 2004 Act) or a category 2 hazard (s.21 (1)) exists on any residential premises, and where no management order is in force in relation to those premises.

The order will specify the prohibition or prohibitions imposed upon the use of the premises (s.20 (2) of the 2004 Act). Furthermore a prohibition order needs to state, amongst other things, whether it is made in respect of a category 1 or 2 hazard (that is, made pursuant to s.20 or s. 21 of the 2004 Act), the nature of the hazard and the residential premises on which it exists, the premises in relation to which prohibitions are imposed along with any remedial action which the authority consider would, if taken in relation to the hazard, result in their revoking the order (s.22 (2)).

For the content of prohibition orders see s.22 of the 2004 Act.

Similar to the offence in s. 30 (1) of the 2004 Act in respect of failing to comply with improvement notices, the offence in s. 32 (1) applies where a person knows that a prohibition order has become 'operative'. By s. 24 (2) of the 2004 Act a prohibition order generally becomes operative at the end of the period of 28 days beginning with the date specified in the notice as the date on which it is made, but again this is subject to exceptions (see s.24 (3) to (5) of the 2004 Act).

Again, the offence in s. 32 (1) of the 2004 Act only applies for the purposes of s. 40 (3) of the HPA 2016 in relation to housing in England let by a landlord if the prohibition order was given in respect of a hazard on the premises let by the landlord (as opposed, for example, to common parts). Again, see s.40 (4) of the HPA 2016.

See also paragraphs 1 and 2 of Schedule 2 of the 2004 Act for the rules relating to the people on whom the authority must serve copies.

(5) Control of or management of unlicensed HMO

The fifth offence in s. 40 (3) of the HPA 2016 is contained in s.72 (1) of the 2004 Act :

> *"(1) A person commits an offence if he is a person having control of or managing an HMO which is required to be licensed under this Part...but is not so licensed."*

This offence regularly forms the basis of applications to the FTT for RROs under the HPA 2016, as does the similar offence contained in s. 95 (1) of the 2004 Act (control or management of an unlicensed 'house').

The offence in s. 95 (1) is discussed below, and because of its similarity much of what follows in respect of s. 72 (1) will be relevant to it also.

These are the essential elements of the offence in s. 72 (1) of the 2004 Act.

(i) A 'house in multiple occupation'

For the meaning of 'HMO' – that is, a house in multiple occupation – s.77 and, in particular, sections 254 to 259 of the 2004 Act are the starting points.

Section 254 (1) of the 2004 Act effectively provides five routes by which a building or a part of a building will be an HMO, unless exempted by Schedule 14.

In this respect there exists 'the standard test' (s. 254 (2)), 'the self-contained flat test' (s. 254 (3)), and'the converted building test' (s. 254 (4)).

Further, a building or part of a building will also be an HMO where:

- there is in force an HMO declaration made by an LHA under s. 255 of the 2004 Act in respect of it. See both sections 255 and 256;

- it is a 'converted block of flats to which s.257 applies' (s. 254 (1) (e) of the 2004 Act). In general terms, this means a building or part of a building which has been converted into and consists of self-contained flats in respect of which certain building standards relating to the conversion were not met (and are still not met) and where less than two-thirds of the self-contained flats are owner-occupied. See s.257 of the 2004 Act.

As for the 'tests', by s. 254 (2) of the 2004 Act a building or a part of a building meets the standard test if:

(a) it consists of one or more units of living accommodation not consisting of a self-contained flat or flats (see below for the meaning of 'self-contained flat');

(b) the living accommodation is occupied by persons who do not form a single household (see below in respect of 'persons forming a single household');

(c) the living accommodation is occupied by those persons as their only or main residence or they are to be treated as so occupying it;

(d) their occupation of the living accommodation constitutes the only use of that accommodation;

(e) rents are payable or other consideration is to be provided in respect of at least one of those persons' occupation of the living accommodation; and

(f) two or more of the households who occupy the living accommodation share one or more basic amenities or the living accommodation is lacking in one or more basic amenities.

By s.254 (3) of the 2004 Act a part of a building meets the self-contained flat test if:

(a) It consists of a self-contained flat (again, see below for the meaning of self-contained flat); and

(b) The conditions in (b) to (f) in relation to the standard test apply (see immediately above) with references there to the living accommodation to be read as references to the flat.

By s. 254 (4) of the 2004 Act a building or a part of a building meets the converted building test if:

(a) it is a converted building (see below for the meaning of this);

(b) it contains one or more units of living accommodation that do not consist of a self-contained flat or flats (whether or not it also contains any such flat or flats);

(c) the living accommodation is occupied by persons who do not form a single household;

(d) the living accommodation is occupied by those persons as their only or main residence or they are to be treated as so occupying it;

(e) their occupation of the living accommodation constitutes the only use of that accommodation; and

(f) rents are payable or other consideration is to be provided in respect of at least one of those persons' occupation of the living accommodation.

For the above purposes by s. 254 (8) of the 2004 Act:

- a self-contained flat means a separate set of premises (whether or not on the same floor) which forms part of a building either the whole or a material part of which lies above or below some other part of the building and in which a toilet, personal washing facilities and cooking facilities are available for the exclusive use of its occupants;

- a converted building means a building or part of a building consisting of living accommodation in which one or more units of such accommodation have been created since the building or part was constructed.

For these purposes by s. 258 of the 2004 Act persons are to be regarded as not forming a single household unless they are all members of the same family, and a person is a member of the same family as another person if:

- they are married or are civil partners (or live together as if they are a married couple or civil partners); or

- one of them is a 'relative' of the other, meaning a parent, grandparent, child, grandchild, brother, sister, uncle, aunt, nephew, niece or cousin (and a relationship of the half-blood is treated as a relationship of the whole blood and a stepchild of a person is treated as that person's child); or

- one of them is, or is a relative of, one member of a couple and the other is a relative of the other member of the couple, and for these purposes a 'couple' means two persons who are married to or civil partners of each other or live together as such.

See also s.259 in respect of persons treated as occupying premises as their only or main residence and s. 262 (6) for the meaning of 'occupier'.

There are other persons who in certain circumstances may be regarded as forming a single household.

These include persons working or performing certain services of an exclusively domestic nature for a person or people where the living accommodation is supplied by them as part of the consideration for carrying out the work/performing the service and where no rent or other consideration is paid or given in respect of the accommodation.

Such people may include a governess, au pairs, nannies, carers and servants (amongst others).

Circumstances are also prescribed relating to certain adult placement carers in respect of persons receiving care where that person lives with the carer in the same building or part of the building, as well as to certain foster parents.

As this is highly fact-specific, establishing whether or not persons satisfy the above will require careful consideration of the Licensing and

Management of Houses in Multiple Occupation and Other Houses (Miscellaneous Provisions) (England) Regulations 2006/373, in particular Regulations 3 and 4.

(ii) exemptions contained in Schedule 14

Schedule 14 of the 2004 Act provides circumstances in which certain buildings or parts of a building that would not for these purposes be an HMO.

The Schedule includes (a) properties controlled or managed by public sector bodies or certain housing let by registered providers of social housing or specified 'co-operative societies' (b) certain religious buildings (c) buildings regulated otherwise than under the 2004 Act (d) buildings occupied by students where the person managing or having control of the buildings is the educational establishment (i.e halls of residence) (e) certain 'owner-occupied' buildings and (f) buildings or parts of building occupied only by two persons forming two households.

Again, the exemptions in Schedule 14 are detailed so practitioners should refer to the schedule itself when considering whether or not the offence in s. 72 (1) of the 2004 Act may have been committed.

(iii) An HMO which is required to be licensed under Part 2 of the 2004 Act

Establishing that a building or a part of a building was at a particular time an HMO is not the end of the analysis. Section 72 (1) of the 2004 Act makes it clear to which HMOs the offence applies: the offence will be committed by a person if he is a person having control of or managing an HMO which is required to be licensed under Part 2 of the 2004 Act but is not so licensed. It is therefore a matter of establishing whether or not the HMO required by virtue of Part 2 of the 2004 Act a licence and, if it did, whether or not at the material time it had one.[1]

Unless there is in force under s. 62 of the 2004 Act a 'temporary exemption notice' or an interim or final management order under Chapter 1 of Part 4 of the same Act, every HMO that is subject to 'mandatory' or 'additional' licensing must be licensed (s.61(1) & s.55 of the 2004 Act).

'Mandatory licensing'

From 1st October 2018 this applies to an HMO that is occupied by five or more persons living in two or more separate households that satisfies any of the following:

(i) the standard test in s.254 (2) of the 2004 Act;

(ii) the self-contained flat test in s.254(3), but is not a purpose-built flat situated in a block comprising three or more self-contained flats; or

(iii) the converted building test in s.254 (4).

See Article 4 of the Licensing of Houses in Multiple Occupation (Prescribed Description) (England) Order (SI 2018/221).

'Additional licensing'

An LHA also has a power to go beyond the above 'mandatory scheme' and designate an area in its district as being subject to 'additional licensing'. This means that for a period specified any HMO will require

---

1 A licence under Part 2 of the 2004 Act is a licence provided by local housing authorities authorising occupation of the house by not more than a maximum number of households or persons specified in it (s. 62 (2) of the 2004 Act).

a licence if it is an HMO that falls within the description specified in the designation and if it is located within the area covered by it. The designation can cover the whole, or an area, of the LHA's district. See s.56 (1) of the 2004 Act.

(iv) A person having control of or managing an HMO

The next point to consider is: upon whom are these licensing requirements placed? Putting it differently, who is 'a person having control of' or 'a person managing' an HMO for the purposes of s. 72 (1) of the 2004 Act?

Section 263 of the 2004 Act explains both of these:

> *"In* [the 2004 Act] *'person having control', in relation to premises, means (unless the context otherwise requires) the person who receives the rack-rent of the premises (whether on his own account or as agent or trustee of another person), or who would so receive it if the premises were let at a rack-rent."*

A 'rack rent' means a rent which is not less than two-thirds of the full net annual value of the premises (s.263 (2) of the 2004 Act).

As for 'person managing' as referred to in s. 72 (1), s. 263 (3) states that in the 2004 Act this means:

> *"...in relation to premises, the person who, being an owner or lessee of the premises–*
>
> *(a) receives (whether directly or through an agent or trustee) rents or other payments from–*
>
> *(i) in the case of a house in multiple occupation, persons who are in occupation as tenants or licensees of parts of the premises; and*

> *(ii) in the case of a house to which Part 3 applies (see section 79(2)), persons who are in occupation as tenants or licensees of parts of the premises, or of the whole of the premises; or*
>
> *(b) would so receive those rents or other payments but for having entered into an arrangement (whether in pursuance of a court order or otherwise) with another person who is not an owner or lessee of the premises by virtue of which that other person receives the rents or other payments;*
>
> *and includes, where those rents or other payments are received through another person as agent or trustee, that other person."*

The Upper Tribunal's decision in *Cabo v. Dezotti* [2022] UKUT 240 (LC) is an example of someone still being a *'person managing'* for the purposes of s. 263 (3) of the 2004 Act even though they did not receive rent themselves. In *Cabo* this occurred because the landlord had entered into an agreement with a management company. The claim being advanced was that this was a company run by the landlord's estranged husband – and this company was not an owner or lessee but it did, because of the agreement, receive the rent from the tenant in occupation. Because of this fact it did not matter that the landlord herself did not receive the rents (or other payments). She would have received that money but for this agreement and, therefore, the meaning of 'person managing' in s. 263 (3) (b) was satisfied and an RRO made.

The Court of Appeal later dismissed a further appeal brought by the landlord against the Upper Tribunal's decision. That appeal (see [2024] EWCA Civ 1358) sought to challenge the decision that the landlord was indeed the 'landlord' for the purposes of an RRO application because she was an undisclosed principal. It also failed.

This is an important point, however, because who the 'landlord' is will be crucial. As stated already, RROs are orders requiring a landlord to repay an amount of rent (or universal credit), and the FTT has the power to make such an order where a landlord has committed one of the seven offences discussed in this chapter (s. 40 of the HPA 2016).

With this in mind, it is usually clear to see that the landlord is the 'person' for the purposes of the offence in s. 72 (1) (and the similar offence in s.95 (1) discussed below). A simple landlord and tenant relationship is normally a chain comprising just two links: a landlord down to a tenant. However, establishing that it is the 'landlord' that has committed these licensing offences may be more complicated where the landlord and tenant 'chain' has a number of links to it.

An example of this is *Cottam v. Lowe Management Ltd* [2023] UKUT 306 (LC)). An NHS clinical commissioning group and freeholder had, via a charitable trust, let its premises to a property guardian company who would arrange for 'guardians' to occupy the premises with the aim of preventing squatting or vandalism. An important part of the case was that this property guardian company did not pay rent to the NHS commissioning group. That company in turn appointed the respondent ("LML") who then granted licenses to the guardians to share occupation of the premises. It was these guardians who made the application for the RRO against LML on the basis that it (LML) was the person having control of or managing the unlicensed HMO (that is, the offence in s. 72 (1)) of the 2004 Act).

LML relied upon Schedule 14 of the 2004 Act arguing that the premises were not an HMO because it was, LML said, the NHS commissioning group (and this was a health service body) that was the person having control of or managing the property (see above summary of exemptions in Schedule 14 of the 2004 Act).

In disagreeing with the FTT the Upper Tribunal determined that the NHS commissioning group, receiving no rent from the property guardian company, was not pursuant to s.263 (1) of the 2004 Act 4 a '*person in control of the premises.*'

If premises are currently let at a rack-rent then the phrase '*person in control*' is the person who receives that rack-rent. However, the Upper Tribunal found that: "*...the person* 'who would so receive it if the premises were let at a rack-rent' *is not a person who might have let at a rack-rent but has in fact let the property (or part of it) for less than a rack-rent; it is the person who as things stand at present, with all the current lettings in place, could if they chose grant a lease at a rack-rent. It is therefore not the freeholder if the freeholder has already let the property, or parts of it, at less than a rack-rent...*" (Judge Elizabeth Cooke, *Cottam v. Lowe Management Ltd* [2023] UKUT 306 (LC)).

Defences applicable to s. 72 (1) of the 2004 Act

Although it is not a requirement to prove the landlord knew that the premises required a licence ((see *R (on the application of Mohamed) v. Waltham Forest LBC* [2020] EWHC 1084 (Admin)) there are defences contained in s. 72 (4) (a) and (b) of the 2004 Act.

Firstly, it is a defence if it can be shown by a defendant that at the material time a notification had been duly given to the LHA under s. 62 (1). Such a notification is in respect of the house notifying the LHA of the intention of the person having control of or managing the HMO to take particular steps with a view to securing that it is no longer required to be licensed (see s.72 (4) (a) of the 2004 Act).

Secondly, it will be a defence if it can be shown that an application for a licence had been duly made in respect of the house under section 63 of the 2004 Act (see s. 72 (4) (b) of the 2004 Act).

However, for the giving of the notification to the LHA under s. 62 (1) or the making of an application for a licence under s. 63 to amount to a defence each has to be 'effective' when given or made (as the case may be).

'Effective' means that the notice or the application has not been withdrawn and either:

- the LHA has yet to decide whether to serve a 'temporary exemption notice' under s. 62 (2) or grant a licence; or

- if they have decided not to serve an exemption notice or grant a licence then either:

    - the time-limit for appealing the LHA's decision has not expired; or

    - the appeal has yet to be determined and has not been withdrawn.

See s. 72 (8) & (9) of the 2004 Act. See also the discussion below in respect of the similar provisions relating to the offence in s. 95 (1) of the 2004 Act.

The defence of 'reasonable excuse'

There is a further defence – of much broader potential application – contained in s.72 (5) of the 2004 Act. This provides that it will be a defence if a person can show that he had a reasonable excuse for having control of or managing the house that was required to be licensed under Part 2 of the 2004 Act but was not.

This is not the same as there having existed at the material time a reasonable excuse for not applying for an HMO licence (see *Palmview Estates Ltd v. Thurrock Council* [2021] EWCA Civ 1871 for an illustration of the difference).

Whether or not there is a 'reasonable excuse' will depend upon the circumstances of each case; the defence is frequently advanced by landlords before the FTT when responding to applications for RROs.

One common argument is that the giving of the management of the premises to a competent property agent should amount to a reasonable excuse for not having a licence if the agent did not inform the landlord of the need to have one. However, in *Aytan v. Moore* [2002] UKUT 27 (LC) the Upper Tribunal set a high bar in this respect by saying that a landlord's reliance upon an agent will rarely give rise to a defence of reasonable excuse. It was said that "at the very least" the landlord would need to show (i) that there was a contractual obligation on the part of the agent to keep the landlord informed of licensing requirements (ii) there would need to be evidence that the landlord had good reason to rely on the competence and experience of the agent and (iii) there would generally be a need to show that there was a reason why the landlord could not inform themself of the licensing requirements without relying upon an agent (the example given being where a landlord lived abroad).

The defence of reasonable excuse has been established where a landlord had been told by a local authority when initially letting the property that an HMO licence was not needed at that time – but that she would be informed by them if that position changed. There having been no notification (despite it later becoming a requirement to have a licence) there was in that particular case a reasonable excuse for not having one. See *D'Costa v. Andrea* [2021] UKUT 144 (LC).

D'Costa was relied upon by the respondent landlord in *Marigold v Wells* [2023] UKUT 33 (LC). Before the FTT the landlord had said that he had been told by a representative of the local authority during a telephone call regarding an HMO licence that one was not needed – but that a scheme was soon to come into force and, when it did, he would be contacted again. As he said that he was not contacted, the FTT had said that he had a reasonable excuse. The Upper Tribunal set this aside and remitted the matter back to the FTT for further consideration. This was because the FTT had erred in not considering whether it was reasonable for the landlord to continue *not* to check if a licence was required over time in circumstances where he had been told that an additional licencing scheme would soon come into force.

In *Ojukwu v. Onuoha* [2024] UKUT 313 (LC) the Upper Tribunal, allowing an appeal, remitted the case back to the FTT because it had not adequately considered the possible application of the defence of reasonable excuse in the context of a contention that the appropriate LHA's website had stated that a licence was not required when, in fact, it was.

In *Kumar v Kolev* [2024] UKUT 255 (LC) a freehold owner of a property had let it to a company who had, in turn, granted sub-tenancies to tenants of individual rooms in the property. The sub-tenants applied for an RRO against the freehold owner because, despite a covenant in the tenancy agreement between the company and the freehold owner limiting the occupation to no more than four people, the company had permitted five people to occupy – making it an HMO that required a licence.

The Upper Tribunal decided, amongst other things, that the freehold owner had a reasonable excuse for not having a licence. The relevant factors were that he had let the whole property to an apparently reputable tenant (the company) on the recommendation of an agent whose judgment he trusted; that he had included a provision in the tenancy agreement with the company that the property was not to be made available to more than four occupiers; that the apparently reputable tenant company had breached that provision without the freeholder's knowledge; and that for part of the period during which the offence was said to have been committed the freeholder had been abroad and, at the end of the period, was unable to return due to Covid restrictions.

In *Newell v Abbott* [2024] UKUT 181 (LC) the Upper Tribunal again considered whether a landlord who was unaware of the need to obtain a licence had a reasonable excuse for having control of an unlicensed property. This case concerned the similar offence in s. 95 (1) of the 2004 Act relating to the licensing of 'part 3 houses' (discussed below). The landlord's defence was based upon a number of factors including simply being unaware of the licensing scheme, the LHA sending correspondence to the landlord about the scheme to an old address, the tenants not passing on post to the landlord and a council officer not replying to an email and telephone call from the landlord that he had made once it was known that the council officer wanted to speak to him about the property. The defence of reasonable excuse was, however, rejected. It was said that the FTT will need to consider (i) the standard of a reasonable landlord or property manager and (ii) the particular characteristics of the individual who has not achieved those standards. The Upper Tribunal said that, to be reasonable, an excuse must be objectively reasonable, and the standards which landlords are generally expected to achieve will be an important measure of what is objectively reasonable in a particular case.

As the above cases illustrate, the existence of the defence is highly fact-dependent.

The defence of reasonable excuse will have to be proven to the civil standard (balance of probabilities) by the respondent landlord. See *IR Management Services Limited v Salford City Council* [2020] UKUT 81 (LC).

(6). Control or management of an unlicensed house

The sixth offence in s. 40 (3) of the HPA 2016 is contained in s. 95 (1) of the 2004 Act and, as with the offence discussed above contained in s. 72 (1), concerns a failure to obtain a licence in respect of certain premises.

Section 95 (1) of the 2004 Act reads:

> *"(1) A person commits an offence if he is a person having control of or managing a house which is required to be licensed under this Part (see section 85(1)) but is not so licensed."*

See above for the meaning of '*a person having control of*' (s. 263 (1)) and '*person managing*' (s. 263 (3)).

(i) A 'house'

There are clear similarities with the offence under s. 72 (1) of the 2004 Act; the key difference is that the offence in s.95 (1) relates to certain types of 'houses' – rather than certain types of 'HMOs'.

A 'house' is for these purposes defined more broadly than the word might be understood generally in that it means "...*a building or part of a building consisting of one or more dwellings*..." (s.99 of the 2004 Act).

Part of such a building would therefore include a flat.

(ii) a house which is required to be licensed under Part 3 of the 2004 Act

As with the HMO offence in s. 72 (1), it is not just a matter of identifying whether the building in question constitutes a 'house' as just defined. The next key question is: what is meant in s. 95 (1) of the 2004 Act by "...*a house which is required to be licensed under this Part*..."?

As stated above the offence in s. 72 (1) is in Part 2 of the 2004 Act, and Part 2 includes the two schemes of licensing mentioned already: mandatory licensing and additional licensing.

The offence in s. 95 (1), in contrast, comes under Part 3 of the 2004 Act, which contains a third licensing scheme of certain residential accommodation: selective licensing.

In this respect s. 85 (1) of the 2004 Act requires every "Part 3 house" to be licensed unless:

- it is an HMO to which Part 2 applies (see s.55(2)); or
- a 'temporary exemption notice' is in force in relation to it under s. 86; or
- a management order is in force in relation to it under Chapter 1 or 2 of Part 4 of the 2004 Act.

For these purposes a "Part 3 house" is:

- a house that is in an area that is for the time being designated by an LHA as subject to selective licensing; and

- the whole of it is occupied either:

    (i) under a single tenancy or licence that is not an exempt tenancy or licence; or

    (ii) under two or more tenancies or licences in respect of different dwellings contained in it, none of which is an exempt tenancy or licence.

See s.85 (5) and s. 79 (2) of the 2004 Act.

The exemptions for tenancies and licences referred to above concern the status of the entity granting the tenancy or the licence. In broad terms they apply to providers of social housing. Put differently, these tenancies or licenses granted by such providers are exempt from the licensing requirements. These exemptions are found in s. 79 (3) of the 2004 Act.

Furthermore, in England there are additional tenancies or licences exempt from these licensing requirements by virtue of the Selective Licensing of Houses (Specified Exemptions) (England) Order 2006 (SI 2006/370). Examples include business tenancies, tenancies of agricultural land and a tenancy or licence of a house managed or controlled by certain public bodies, including LHAs and a health service body.

By s. 80 (1) of the 2004 Act an LHA has the power to designate the whole area of its district or an area in its district as subject to selective licensing. Such an area may only be designated where certain requirements are met (see s. 80 (1) of the 2004 Act).

Focusing on this offence in the context of applications to the FTT for an RRO the important point is that, in a way similar to additional licensing discussed above, a particular LHA may by designation select a certain geographical area within which, and for a specified time, any Part 3 house will require a licence.

(iii) Defences applicable to s. 95 (1) of the 2004 Act

In the context of Part 3 houses defences are contained in s. 95 (3) & (4) (a) of the 2004 Act. They are that:

- The person had a reasonable excuse for having control of or managing the house that was not licensed (despite it being required to be by s.85 (1)). For a discussion of the defence of reasonable excuse see above in the context of s. 72 (5);

- At the material time a notification had been duly given to the LHA in respect of the house under s.62(1) or s.86(1) of the 2004 Act (relating to steps that are intended to be taken with a view to securing that the relevant HMO or house no longer requires a licence); or

- At the material time an application for a licence had been duly made in respect of the house under s. 87 of the 2004 Act.

As discussed above in respect of the offence in s. 72 (1), such a notification or application (as the case may be) has to be 'effective' at the material time. This means that the notification or the application has not been withdrawn and either:

- the authority has not decided whether to serve a 'temporary exemption notice' under s.62 (2) or s.86 (2) or grant a licence (as the case may be) in pursuance of the notification or the application; or

- if it has decided not to do so then either:

    (a) the period in respect of the following has not expired:

        (i) the period for appealing against the decision of the authority not to serve a temporary exemption notice or grant a licence; or

(ii) the period for appealing against a decision of the FTT made on an appeal to it confirming the authority's decision; or

(b) that an appeal has been made to the FTT against the authority's decision, or an appeal has been made against the FTT's decision to confirm the authority's decision, and the appeal has not been determined or withdrawn.

See s.95 (7) to (9) of the 2004 Act.

If the appeal is against the LHA's decision not to serve a temporary exemption notice then the time limit for appealing to the FTT is 28 days (s. 86 (7) of the 2004 Act).

The same time limit applies if the appeal is against the LHA's decision to refuse to grant a licence. In that scenario the FTT may allow such an appeal to be made after this period if it is satisfied that there is a good reason for the failure to appeal before the end of the period and for any delay since then in applying for permission to appeal out of time (see part 3 of Schedule 5 of the 2004 Act, in particular paragraph 33 relevant to the offences in s. 72 (1) and s. 95 (1)). It appears, however, that this power to allow an appeal after the 28-day period is limited only to appeals against a decision to refuse to grant a licence and not to a decision not to serve a temporary exemption notice.

There is no right to appeal to the FTT against an authority's decision not to grant a licence where a banning order is involved. See paragraph 32A of Schedule 5 of the 2004 Act.

(7). Breach of Banning Order

The seventh, and currently final, offence in s. 40 (3) of the HPA 2016 is the only offence that is contained within the HPA 2016 itself, namely the offence in s.21 of the HPA 2016 of breaching a banning order.

By s.14 (1) of the HPA 2016 a 'banning order' is an order that is made by the FTT banning a person from:

(i) letting housing in England;

(ii) engaging in 'English letting agency work' (see s.54 (5) of the HPA 2016);

(iii) engaging in 'English property management work' (see s. 55 (3) of the HPA 2016); or

(iv) doing two or more of those things.

The FTT may make banning orders upon the application of an LHA (as to which see below) against a person who:

(i) has been convicted of a 'banning order offence', and

(ii) was a residential landlord or a property agent at the time the offence was committed (s.16 (1) of the HPA 2016).

There are a number of 'banning order offences' the commission of which, in certain circumstances, will then allow an LHA to apply for a banning order, but it is only in circumstances where the FTT is satisfied that a banning order has been breached that it then, in respect of an application for an RRO, has the power to make an RRO.

As such, it is beyond the scope of this book to consider each of the many 'banning order offences' that may in turn lead to an application for a banning order. Practitioners may, however, wish to consider Regulation 3 of the Housing and Planning Act 2016 (Banning Order Offences) Regulations 2018/216 and the list of offences in its Schedule 1.

See also s.14 (5) of the HPA 2016, which makes an offence under s. 12 of the Tenant Fees Act 2019 a 'banning order offence'.

As stated, the FTT may make a banning order on an application by an LHA in England and, when applying, that authority must comply with s. 15 of the HPA 2016 (see s.16 (2)).

This requires the LHA, before applying for a banning order against a person who has been convicted of a banning order offence, to give that person a notice of intended proceedings informing the person that the LHA is proposing to apply for a banning order (and explaining why), stating the length of each proposed ban and inviting the person to make representations within a period specified in the notice of not less than 28 days (s.15 (3) of the HPA 2016).

The LHA must then consider any representations made and must not in any event apply to the FTT for a banning order before the end of the period specified in the notice. A notice of intended proceedings may not be given after the end of the period of 6 months beginning with the day on which the person was convicted of the offence to which the notice relates.

If an LHA applies for a banning order against a body corporate that has been convicted of a banning order offence, it must also apply for a banning order against any officer who has been convicted of the same offence in respect of the same conduct (s.15 (2) of the HPA 2016).

In deciding whether to make a banning order against a person, and in deciding what order to make, the FTT must consider the seriousness of the offence of which the person has been convicted, any previous convictions that the person has for a banning order offence, whether the person is or has at any time been included in the database of rogue landlords and property agents and the likely effect of the banning order on the person and anyone else who may be affected by the order (s.16 (4) of the HPA 2016).

These are the factors that must be considered in every case, but they are not the only factors that may be taken into account by the FTT.

Although it may not happen often, the Upper Tribunal has held that the FTT may consider spent convictions when deciding whether or not to make a banning order (see *Hussain v London Borough of Newham* [2023] UKUT 287 (LC)).

In *Knapp v. Bristol City Council* [2023] UKUT 118 (LC) the Upper Tribunal refused to interfere with a banning order made by the FTT against a landlord that, amongst other things, prohibited them from the letting of housing for a period of five years. It also upheld the FTT's order to ban the landlord from both future and existing lettings (the FTT having suspended the ban for six months in respect of existing tenancies).

In summary, it can be seen that there are a number of hurdles that will have to be cleared before an applicant may, relying upon s. 21 (1) of the HPA 2016, seek an RRO for breach of a banning order.

Changes proposed by the Renters' Rights Bill

Additional qualifying offences

The Renters' Rights Bill shall add – or, at the time of writing, is very likely to add – to the seven offences in the table in s.40 (3) of the HPA 2016 discussed in this chapter, and it would make significant changes to the RRO regime in the HPA 2016 generally.

The current proposals in the Bill would add a further six offences – with the seven current offences in s. 40 (3) of the HPA 2016 discussed in this chapter remaining. If the Bill was passed in this form it would result in a total of 13 offences, and considering the size of the current Government's Parliamentary majority it is likely that they and other important parts in the Bill will become law.

The following is a summary of the proposed additional offences for the purposes of s. 40 (3) of the HPA 2016 and the legislation creating those additional offences:

- Housing Act 1988 (s.16J(1): knowingly or recklessly misusing a possession ground;
- Housing Act 1988 (s.16J(2)): breach of restriction on letting or marketing dwelling-house;
- Housing Act 1988 (s.16J(3)): tenancy reform: continuing breaches;
- Renters' Rights Act 2024 (s.65(1)): landlord redress schemes: continuing breaches;
- Renters' Rights Act 2024 (s.90 (1)): private rented sector database: provision of false or misleading information;
- Renters' Rights Act 2024 (s.90 (2) (but only if the penalty imposed relates to a breach of a requirement imposed by section 80(3)): private rented sector database: continuing breaches.

As a result of the above practitioners must ensure they consider the latest version of s. 40 (3) of the HPA 2016.

A widening of the licensing offences in s. 72 (1) & s. 95 (1) of the 2004 Act

In addition to adding to the offences the commission of which would empower the FTT to make an RRO, the Government is also wanting to broaden the scope of the two offences most commonly committed in the context of applications for RROs.

The proposed amendments would mean that each licensing offence (HMOs re s. 72 (1) and Part 3 houses re. s95 (1)) could be committed by:

- any person having control of or managing the HMO or house; and

- any person who is the landlord or licensor in relation to a person occupying the HMO or the house under a tenancy or licence; and

- with the aim of making superior landlords subject to RROs in mind, any person who as landlord under a tenancy or licensor under a licence to occupy has an estate or interest in, or a right in relation to, the HMO or the house that is superior (whether directly or indirectly) to the estate, interest or right of any such person.

In relation to the first two points, there will be inserted comparable defences of 'reasonable excuse' as to those in s. 72 (5) and s. 95 (4) (a) currently that will be applicable to these newly-formulated offences.

In respect of the superior landlord addition, three specific defences are proposed in that it will be a defence if the person can prove that they:

- did not know, and had a reasonable excuse for not knowing, that the building or part of the building concerned was an HMO or a house; or

- took all reasonably practicable steps to ensure that the HMO or the house was licensed; or

- had some other reasonable excuse for failing to ensure that the HMO or the house was so licensed.

Summary

- Currently there are seven gateways ('offences') that permit an application to be made to the FTT for an RRO;

- They have to be proven beyond reasonable doubt, but a 'conviction' is not a requirement;

- Some of these are more serious than others, with the two most common offences dealt with by the FTT being two offences relating to controlling or managing certain residential accommodation without a licence in circumstances where a licence was required;

- At the time of writing important additional offences are proposed – with the seven that currently exist remaining – along with a proposed broadening of the scope of the two licensing offences currently in section s72 (1) and s. 95 (1) of the 2004 Act.

CHAPTER THREE

AGAINST WHOM CAN A RENT REPAYMENT ORDER BE MADE?

Introduction

Putting the above question differently: who should be the person(s) or entity named as the respondent(s) on the application seeking an order for the repayment of the rent?

Who should be liable for the repayment of the rent?

This chapter focuses on these questions and, in particular, discusses some of the reasons why the question is not as easy to answer as it might, at first glance, seem to be.

In particular, the chapter addresses situations where there is a 'chain' of interests involving both an immediate landlord and a superior landlord, as well as the position with directors of corporate landlords.

Of course, identification of 'the landlord' in respect of a particular residential letting is plainly not the only qualifying condition for the purposes of applying for and obtaining a rent repayment order ("an RRO") – the aim of the RRO regime being to punish 'rogue landlords'.

An RRO is an order that may be made not simply against any landlord but against a landlord that has first committed a particular housing-related 'offence'. These offences – effectively, the grounds for seeking an RRO – are the subject of Chapter 2.

This chapter, in contrast, deals with issues that may arise when seeking to identify the 'landlord' and outlines the applicable statutory provisions and key case law.

The chapter ends by looking at some of the important proposals contained in the Renters' Rights Bill in respect of this question (against whom may RROs be made?) As will be seen, the Bill is likely to lead to significant changes to the current law.

Against whom can a Rent Repayment Order be made?

The simple answer to this is question is 'the landlord'.

In most cases it will be clear who this is, most likely from the parties' dealings throughout the letting and from various documentation (including, of course, the written tenancy agreement itself, if there is one).

However, what if a landlord has let premises to a tenant who in turn lets those same premises out to a number of sub-tenants thereby creating a chain of proprietary interests? In this scenario – which is a central feature of 'rent-to-rent' arrangements – there will be three links to that chain (if not more): the residential occupying sub-tenants, their immediate landlord and the landlord superior to that landlord.

If standing in the shoes of one of those sub-tenants, who is the correct landlord for the purposes of making an application for an RRO? Who should they be seeking the repayment of rent from? The sub-tenant's immediate landlord or the superior landlord?

'The landlord'

When looking to identify the correct respondent to an application for an RRO under Chapter 4 of Part 2 of the HPA 2016 the starting point is s.

40 (1) & (2) of the HPA 2016 because this section contains the key definitions underpinning its RRO regime:

> *"(1)* [Chapter 4] *confers power on the First-tier Tribunal to make a rent repayment order where a landlord has committed an offence to which this Chapter applies.*
>
> *(2) A rent repayment order is an order requiring the landlord under a tenancy of housing in England to—*
>
> *(a) repay an amount of rent paid by a tenant, or*
>
> *(b) pay a local housing authority an amount in respect of a relevant award of universal credit paid (to any person) in respect of rent under the tenancy."*

As can be seen the power that is given to the First-tier Tribunal (Property Chamber) ("the FTT") to make an RRO applies where 'a landlord' has committed one of a number of offences that are listed in s.40 (3) of the HPA 2016 (see Chapter 2).

This is straightforward: the landlord has committed the offence and the landlord can be made to repay rent (or a relevant award universal credit) as a result.

The HPA 2016 does not define 'landlord' for the purposes of s. 40 or Chapter 4 more generally. However, the Upper Tribunal (Lands Chamber) ("the Upper Tribunal") and the higher courts have considered this question.

Rakusen v. Jepsen & superior landlords

The Supreme Court in *Rakusen v. Jepsen* [2023] UKSC 9 made it clear that an RRO under the HPA 2016 could only be made against a tenant's immediate landlord and not any superior landlord. Or, as the Supreme Court put it:

> "*...an RRO cannot be made against a superior landlord, that is, a landlord higher up the chain of tenancies than the immediate landlord under the tenancy which generates the relevant rent.*"

The case involved three tenants who applied to the FTT for an RRO in respect of rent paid by them when letting rooms in a flat in north London. They alleged that the flat they had occupied required an HMO licence but did not have one and they were therefore entitled to an RRO.

However, the person against whom the applicants sought the RRO – the respondent to the application – was not the applicants' immediate landlord but a superior landlord, Mr Rakusen. He had let the whole of the flat to a company which then let individual rooms in the flat to the three applicants. The respondent to the RRO application (Mr Rakusen) was, therefore, a superior landlord. To employ the chain analogy used by the Supreme Court, he was a superior landlord who was one link above the company who had granted the applicants their tenancies of the rooms.

As such the respondent superior landlord applied to the FTT to strike out the application against him for an RRO on the basis that he was not the applicants' immediate landlord and, therefore, the FTT had no power to make the order against him.

The FTT refused to strike out the application. On appeal, the Upper Tribunal also found in favour of the applicant tenants. Those tribunals were of the view that the FTT did have the power to make an RRO against a superior landlord of premises that had been let to the applicant tenants, as well as the immediate landlord.

Mr Rakusen appealed the Upper Tribunal's decision (see [2020] UKUT 298 (LC)) to the Court of Appeal who, in contrast, found that the FTT had no such power in respect of 'superior landlords' (the Court of Appeal's judgment is reported at [2021] EWCA Civ 1150).

The tenants appealed the Court of Appeal's decision to the Supreme Court.

The Supreme Court in dismissing the tenants' appeal and deciding that 'a landlord' for the purposes of RROs in the HPA 2016 meant only the tenants' immediate landlord said:

> *"This straightforward interpretation links the landlord with the tenancy that generates the relevant rent. It renders it artificial and unnatural to construe the opening words of section 40(2) as referring to any landlord other than the landlord under the tenancy which generates the relevant rent, that is the rent to be repaid under section 40(2)(a) and the rent in respect of which the universal credit is paid under section 40(2)(b). It excludes a superior landlord because it is not the "landlord under" the tenancy which generates the rent."*

Therefore, the Supreme Court dismissed the applicant tenants' appeal on the basis that the superior landlord could not be liable for an RRO.

As stated below, however, the Renters' Rights Bill (2024-25) proposes to reverse the Supreme Court's decision in *Rakusen* so that a superior landlord could be held liable.

Seeking an RRO against directors of a corporate landlord

A similarly important issue arose in *Kaszowska v. White* [2022] UKUT 11 (LC). This was an appeal to the Upper Tribunal challenging a decision by the FTT that it could not make an RRO against a managing director of a corporate landlord.

The argument made by the applicant tenants was that the individual in question, although not the landlord himself, was a managing director of the company that was the landlord. Moreover, that person had also – along with the corporate landlord – committed the offence that was being relied upon as the basis of the RRO application (being in control of an unlicensed HMO). This was because where this offence is committed by a body corporate is proved to have been committed with the consent or connivance of a director then that person as well as the corporate body commits the offence (s. 251 (1) of the Housing Act 2004).

The Upper Tribunal held, however, that this provision only took things so far. Establishing whether or not a director of a company that was a landlord had also committed the offence along with the corporate landlord was not an answer to the question of against whom applications for RROs may be made.

That answer was simply: the landlord.

Two important points were made by the Upper Tribunal in *Kaszowska* in deciding that no RRO could be made against a director of a corporate landlord.

Firstly, as was made clear by both the Court of Appeal and later the Supreme Court in *Rakusen,* s.40 (2) of the HPA 2016 states in brief but simple terms that an RRO is an order that requires the landlord under a tenancy of housing in England to repay an amount of rent paid by a tenant. The Upper Tribunal at paragraphs 22 and 23 of its decision in *Kaszowska* said that this was in contrast to who may in fact commit the offences listed in s. 40 (3) that allow an application for an RRO to be made: the commission of those offences was not limited to 'the landlord' but could be committed by property agents, a superior landlord, agents or in the case of the offences of violence for securing entry and unlawful eviction or harassment, by persons who have no connection to the landlord.

These offences are covered in Chapter 2.

Secondly, repayment by someone other than the landlord who received the rent was not part of the RRO regime. As stated, s. 40 (2) of the HPA 2016 defines an RRO as an order requiring a landlord to "repay" rent received from the tenant. The director of the corporate landlord had not directly received the rent from the tenants – that rent had been paid to the corporate landlord.

In *Kumar v. Kolev* [2024] UKUT 255 (LC) the Upper Tribunal discharged an RRO initially made by the FTT against the registered freehold proprietor of a house in London because that person was not the immediate landlord nor had he received rent from the occupying tenants.

In *Kumar* the freeholder had let his house to a company for a monthly rent of £2600. That company, in turn, granted sub-tenancies of the rooms in the house to five people (including the three applicants seeking the RRO). This was contrary to a covenant the company had given to the freeholder to "not permit more than four occupants to reside in the Property at any one time for the duration of the Tenancy". It was this fact that meant the house amounted to an HMO that required – but did not have – a licence.

Additionally, the terms of three of the sub-tenancies were longer than the term given to the company by the freeholder. This meant that the purported grant of the sub-tenancies by the company was an assignment by operation of law of the company's tenancy with the freeholder – thereby making the sub-tenants the direct tenants of the freeholder. It was this that was used as the basis for arguing that the 'immediate landlord requirement', as reiterated by the Supreme Court in *Rakusen*, was satisfied.

The occupying sub-tenants, however, continued to pay the company rent and the company, in turn, continued to pay rent to the freeholder.

The Upper Tribunal found that the FTT had no jurisdiction to make the RRO against the freeholder and discharged it. He was not the immediate landlord, none of the parties having intended that their previous relationships were to change as a result of the assignment by operation of law and, vitally, he had not received any rent from the occupying sub-tenants (only from the company).

In any event, the Upper Tribunal found that the freeholder would have had a defence of 'reasonable excuse' for the purposes of s. 72 (5) of the Housing Act 2004. The Upper Tribunal said that the freeholder had been entitled to rely upon a number of relevant matters in this respect:

> *"...that he had let the whole property to an apparently reputable tenant on the recommendation of an agent whose judgment he trusted; secondly, that he had included a provision in the tenancy agreement that the property was not to be made available to more than four occupiers (and so would not be an HMO required to be licensed); thirdly, that the apparently reputable tenant had breached that provision without Mr Kumar's knowledge; and finally, that for part of the period during which the offence was said to have been committed, 20 September 2019 to 1 April 2020, he had been abroad and, at the end of the period, was unable to return due to Covid restrictions."*

It could be said that the decision in *Kumar* sensibly looked to the reality of the relationships in that despite the assignment of the company's interest by operation of law the occupants kept paying rent to that company and that company, to the freeholder.

Cabo v. Dezotti [2024] EWCA Civ 1358 is an important reminder that the law may look beyond the name inserted on the written agreement when trying to identify who the 'landlord' is for the purposes of making an application for an RRO.

In *Cabo* an argument by the property owner that it had been wrong to make an RRO against her because she should not been treated as 'the landlord' – the assertion being that she had given all rights to a limited company owned by her husband and it was that company that had contracted with the occupant – was rejected. This was because the limited company had the requisite authority from the property owner to enter into that agreement and, further, the company was intending to act on the property owner's behalf when it did so. As a result, the company was an agent of the property owner and she was an undisclosed principal.

Therefore, she was also the landlord against whom an RRO could be made.

Changes proposed by the Renters' Rights Bill 2024–25

The Renters' Rights Bill is, at the time of writing, going through Parliament. As such the precise nature of the changes it is likely to make to the RRO regime in the HPA 2016 are currently unclear; however, that changes will be made and, generally speaking, that they will be in the form contained in the Bill (or similar to) is highly likely.

What follows is a summary of the likely amendments to the RRO regime in the HPA 2016 relevant to this chapter, but because the Bill is at the time of writing going through Parliament it is vital that practitioners ensure that they are referring to the latest version of the HPA 2016 that is subject to any relevant amendments.

The overall policy direction demonstrated by the elements of the Renters' Rights Bill relating to RROs is clear: to continue to employ and expand the RRO scheme as a means of improving housing standards and discouraging those who choose not to comply from letting residential property at all.

In relation to the issues discussed in this chapter, the Bill proposes two important amendments to Chapter 4 of the HPA 2016.

RROs to be permitted against 'superior landlords'

As stated, the Supreme Court in *Rakusen* confirmed that an RRO under the HPA 2016 may only be made against the applicant tenant's immediate landlord.

One argument against this conclusion raised in the case related to how this conclusion might allow landlords to avoid liability and sidestep the penalties thereby undermining the scheme itself: a rogue landlord looking to avoid future sanctions such as RROs could grant a short term tenancy to a company with no assets – aside from that tenancy – meaning the applicants would almost certainly never be able to enforce the RRO (an amount payable to a tenant or an LHA under an RRO is recoverable as a debt: s. 47 (1) of the HPA 2016).

This argument was rejected by the Supreme Court simply because of the clear wording of s. 40 (2) of the HPA 2016, but the Court did note at paragraph 43 of its judgment that its interpretation would have an impact on the effectiveness of RROs:

> *"Having said all that, we accept that the interpretation we take renders RROs less effective than they perhaps could be if they were to be made available against superior landlords. But in our view that development would undermine the clear definition of an RRO, as set out in section 40(2) of the 2016 Act, and would therefore require new legislation. In other words, if this is thought to be a problem any reform would be a matter for Parliament and cannot be achieved through a distorted interpretation of the relevant provisions in the 2016 Act."*

The relevant proposal in the Renters' Rights Bill at the time of writing would reverse the effect of *Rakusen.* The key definitions within s.40 of the HPA 2016 – the section at the heart of the *Rakusen* decision – would if changed as proposed make clear that the FTT's power to make an RRO against a landlord who has committed an offence listed in s. 40 (3) would also apply where the offence has been committed by any superior landlord in relation to such a tenancy.

It is further proposed that there would be added to s.52 of the HPA 2016, which deals with the interpretation of Chapter 4, confirmation that in respect of RRO applications made against a superior landlord:

- references to the landlord in Chapter 4 are to be read as references to the superior landlord; and

- housing in relation to which the person in question is a superior landlord is to be treated for the purposes of Chapter 4 as let by that person.

The guidance issued by the Ministry of Housing, Communities and Local Government, "*Guide to the Renters' Rights Bill*" (updated 26th September 2024), states that the Government is seeking to introduce these legislative changes – extending RROs to superior landlords and company directors – to ensure criminal rent-to-rent arrangements can be properly held to account.

Expanding the meaning of a 'Rent Repayment Order'

The scope of RROs is also likely to be increased by changing the reference to 'Rent Repayment Orders' in s. 40 (2) of the HPA 2016.

Currently s. 40 (2) refers to an RRO as being an order requiring the landlord under a tenancy to "*repay*" an amount of rent paid by a tenant; the FTT is to focus on who the tenant paid the rent to.

The current proposal in the Renters' Rights Bill, however, would widen the impact of the provision by defining an RRO not as an order requiring the '*repayment*' of rent paid by a tenant but simply as an order requiring the landlord to '*pay*' a tenant an amount in respect of rent paid by or on behalf of the tenant.

As stated above, the reference in s. 40 (2) to an RRO being an order requiring a landlord to "*repay*" rent paid by a landlord was a key reason why the application for an RRO in *Kumar* failed. If such an amendment was made to s.40 (2) then an application by a tenant could be made against a superior landlord in circumstances where they had not directly paid that person rent.

RROs against more than one landlord & directors of corporate landlords

The Renters' Rights Bill is also likely to add a new s.51A to the HPA 2016 so as to reverse the decision in *Kaszowska v. White* [2022] UKUT 11 (LC) discussed above. The change is likely to ensure amongst other things that where a corporate landlord has committed an offence (those contained in s. 40 (3) of the HPA 2016) with the consent or connivance of a senior office holder of the company, such as a director, then that person as well as the company will be treated as having committed the offence and references to 'landlord' in Chapter 4 will include that person e.g the director.

In this respect the Renters' Rights Bill will include by way of a new s. 46A of the HPA 2016 provision for an RRO to be made against more than one landlord but the RRO must provide for the landlords to be jointly and severally liable for the amount.

Summary

- currently an RRO can only be made against a tenant's immediate landlord where that person has committed one of the applicable offences. RROs cannot be made against superior landlords who have themselves granted a lease to the applicant tenant's landlord;

- additionally as an RRO is an order that requires a landlord to "repay" rent paid by a tenant, an application cannot currently be brought against a landlord unless that landlord was paid that rent by the tenant, which in turn excludes applications for RROs against directors of companies that are landlords;

- it is clear that the Government feels that the decisions discussed in this chapter lead to an unwanted and unfair narrowing of the scope of the orders;

- proposals in the Renters' Rights Bill will therefore likely make significant changes to who may be made to pay an RRO.

CHAPTER FOUR

DETERMINING THE AMOUNT OF RENT REPAYMENT ORDERS

Introduction

Assuming that the application for the rent repayment order ("RRO") has been brought in time and relates to the correct parties, to get to the issue of the amount of an RRO the First-tier Tribunal (Property Chamber) ("the FTT") must be satisfied:

- Beyond reasonable doubt that one of the prescribed seven offences listed in the table in s.40 (3) of the Housing and Planning Act 2016 ("the HPA 2016") has been committed by a landlord, including being satisfied that there is no relevant defence; and

- That they should make an order. This comes from the fact that by s. 43 (1) of the HPA 2016 the FTT is empowered to make an RRO, but is not obliged to (see 'may make' in s. 43 (1)). However, it would be a very rare case in which the FTT could decide not to exercise its discretion to make an RRO in circumstances where it has found beyond reasonable doubt that a criminal offence has been committed: *London Borough of Newham v Harris* [2017] UKUT 264 (LC).

If these hurdles are cleared, the question then becomes: *'how much?'*

The approach to determining the amount of an RRO

If the application for an RRO is made by a tenant then one must turn to s. 44 of the HPA 2016 to determine the amount.

If the application for an RRO is made by a local housing authority ("LHA") then s.45 of the HPA 2016 determines the amount (see s.43 (3) HPA 2016).

There is also a separate – third – approach to determining the amount that depends upon the landlord's previous conduct as opposed to the status of the applicant, namely cases where the landlord has been convicted of or received a financial penalty in respect of certain (but not all) offences. Where this applies determination of the amount of the RRO is to be in accordance with s. 46 of the HPA 2016 (see s. 43 (3) (c)).

These last two scenarios (applications by LHAs and landlord convictions etc) are addressed briefly below.

As for applications made by LHAs the statutory provisions and approach to determination is in all material respects the same as for applications made by tenants, save that the RRO will relate to a relevant award of universal credit and not rent.

Determining the amount of a rent repayment order where the application is made by a tenant (s. 44 HPA 2016)

Summary:

(i) Identify the maximum that could be awarded;

(ii) Consider deducting certain utilities;

(iii) Assess by comparison the severity of the offence that has been committed; and

(iv) Arrive at an amount having considered the criteria in s.44 (4) of the HPA 2016.

Where the FTT decides to make an RRO in favour of a tenant the amount of the order will be determined in accordance with s.44 of the HPA 2016 (see s.44 (1)).

The approach

In *Acheampong v. Roman* [2022] UKUT 239 (LC) the Upper Tribunal (Lands Chamber) ("the Upper Tribunal") dealt with the approach to be taken by the FTT in deciding how much a landlord should pay by way of an RRO. At paragraphs 18 to 20 Judge Elizabeth Cooke said:

> *"18. It is easy to say what the FTT should not do: it should not take the whole rent (less any payments for utilities) and regard that as the starting point subject only to deductions made in light of the factors in section 44(4) of the 2016 Act.*
>
> *19. What should it do instead?*
>
> *20. The following approach will ensure consistency with the authorities:*
>
> *a. Ascertain the whole of the rent for the relevant period;*
>
> *b. Subtract any element of that sum that represents payment for utilities that only benefited the tenant, for example gas, electricity and internet access. It is for the landlord to supply evidence of these, but if precise figures are not available an experienced tribunal will be able to make an informed estimate.*
>
> *c. Consider how serious this offence was, both compared to other types of offence in respect of which a rent repayment order may be made (and whose relative seriousness can be seen from the relevant maximum sentences on conviction) and compared to other examples of the same type of offence. What proportion of*

> *the rent (after deduction as above) is a fair reflection of the seriousness of this offence? That figure is then the starting point (in the sense that that term is used in criminal sentencing); it is the default penalty in the absence of any other factors but it may be higher or lower in light of the final step:*
>
> *d. Consider whether any deduction from, or addition to, that figure should be made in the light of the other factors set out in section 44(4)"*

Following on from what Fancourt J had said in *Williams v. Parmar* [2021] UKUT 244 (LC), the Upper Tribunal in *Acheampong* made it clear that there was no presumption that the maximum rent would be the starting point for the amount of an RRO – unless, that is, there was a reason to order a lower figure because of the factors in s. 44 (4) of the HPA 2016. It was a 'starting point' only in the sense that the RRO must relate to the maximum rent in some way, but the maximum rent was not to be used as a presumption of what the RRO would be subject to the three factors in s. 44 (4) of the HPA 2016.

In this respect, Judge Elizabeth Cooke in *Acheampong* said at paragraph 17 of her judgment:

> *"There are no rules as to the amount to be repaid; there is no rate card. But it is safe to say that if the landlord is ordered to repay the whole of the rent (after deduction of any payment for utilities), without consideration of the seriousness of the offence, or in a case that is far from the most serious of its kind, it is likely that something has gone wrong and that the FTT has failed to take into consideration a relevant factor".*

The four steps outlined in *Acheampong* will now be considered in turn.

Step One: ascertaining the maximum

The first task will be to identify the maximum amount of any RRO. In other words, ascertain the whole of the rent for the relevant period.

This is because not all rent paid during the occupation will qualify; the legislation is much narrower. The amount of the RRO award must relate to rent paid during a specific period. That period – the 'relevant period' – is established by considering s.44 (2) of the HPA 2016 and the table that it includes. Subsection 2 reads:

> *(2) The amount must relate to rent paid during the period mentioned in the table.*

If the order is made on the ground that the landlord has committed	*the amount must relate to rent paid by the tenant in respect of*
an offence mentioned in row 1 or 2 of the table in section 40(3)	the period of 12 months ending with the date of the offence
an offence mentioned in row 3, 4, 5, 6 or 7 of the table in section 40(3)	a period, not exceeding 12 months, during which the landlord was committing the offence

Put differently, this means:

- If the RRO is made on the ground of violence for securing entry or the ground of eviction or harassment of occupiers, the amount must relate to rent paid by the tenant in respect of the period of 12 months ending with the date of the offence;

- If, however, the RRO is made on the grounds of failure to comply with an improvement notice, failure to comply with a prohibition order etc, being a person in control of or managing an unlicensed HMO or unlicensed house or a breach of a banning order then the amount must relate to rent paid by the tenant in respect of a

> period, not exceeding 12 months, during which the landlord was committing the offence.

In each case the maximum amount of an RRO will be 12 months of rent. See, however, the end of this chapter in respect of proposed changes likely to be made by the Renters' Rights Bill 2024-25 to increase the period to two years.

The amount that the landlord may be required to repay in respect of a period must not exceed the rent paid in respect of that period less any relevant award of universal credit paid (to any person) in respect of rent under the tenancy during that period (see s.44 (3) of the HPA 2016). Furthermore, the amount repayable to a tenant cannot exceed the rent paid during the 12-month period even if the landlord has committed more than one of the seven offences in the above table in respect of that 12-month period (*Ficcara v James* [2021] UKUT 38 (LC)).

A 'relevant award of universal credit' means an award of universal credit the calculation of which included an amount under s. 11 of the Welfare Reform Act 2012 (see s. 52 (1) of the HPA 2016). See also s.51 of the HPA 2016, which confirms that 'housing benefit' under Part 7 of the Social Security Contributions and Benefits Act 1992 is to be included in references to 'universal credit' for these purposes.

Section 44 (2) of the HPA 2016 means that it is necessary to identify when the rent was paid and also the period in respect of which the payment was made.

These two points are well illustrated by the case of *Kowalek v Hassanein Ltd* [2022] EWCA Civ 1041.

The applicant tenants had sought to have included within an RRO award an amount of £2000 paid as rent one day after the landlord had applied for an HMO licence (meaning in law that rent had been paid on a day when the offence in question was not being committed). The tenants argued that although it was paid *during* a period when the offence was not being committed, it was a payment that *related to* rent which fell due when the offence was being committed.

The Court of Appeal (upholding the earlier decision on appeal to the Upper Tribunal [2021 UKUT 143 (LC)) rejected this stating that the maximum amount of an RRO must be determined without regard to rent which, while it might have discharged indebtedness which arose during the period specified in section 44(2), was not paid in that period.

(at the end of this chapter provisions in the Renters' Rights Bill are discussed relating to the proposed change to this requirement by focusing not on when the rent was paid but only on the period in respect of which it was paid).

In terms of working out the amount of an RRO, it might be felt that things would become complicated in cases involving joint tenants.

For example, in *Dowd v. Martins* [2022] UKUT 249 (LC) one of two joint tenants, both having originally applied with others for an RRO against their landlord, had reached an agreement with the landlord and withdrew from the RRO proceedings. The remaining joint tenant sought and was – initially – awarded an RRO that related to all the rent paid. The Upper Tribunal on appeal set this aside and divided the amount to be repaid from the rent paid by the joint tenant that continued with the RRO application by two. It was said that otherwise it would not be fair: the tenant that had settled and withdrew would (behind the scenes) get their rent back despite having withdrawn their application, or the remaining joint tenant would be repaid two persons' rent.

Another issue involving joint tenants concerns applications for an RRO against a landlord by one or some, but not all, of those tenants.

In *Moreira v. Morrison* [2023] UKUT 233 (LC) an application was made by three of five tenants seeking repayment of the whole of the rent on the basis, it was argued, that each had been jointly and severally liable to the respondents for the whole and so the repayment should not be based upon what each tenant actually paid. Agreeing with the FTT, the Upper Tribunal dismissed the appeal. It was said that the amount of the repayment was to be calculated by reference to the amount actually paid by the tenants who made the application.

Before moving on, it may help at this stage for illustrative purposes only to consider an example. We shall assume for the purposes of this example that the monthly rent was £2000 and, after considering the above, the maximum amount of any RRO during the relevant period is £24,000.

This example will be referred to further below.

Step Two: utilities only benefitting the tenant(s)

Once the maximum amount for the relevant period is established the next issue to consider is the cost of certain utilities and decide what, if anything, needs to be deducted from the figure arrived at having undertaken the process considered in step one (in our example, £24,000).

At paragraph 20 of *Acheampong* Judge Elizabeth Cooke said the following:

> *"b. Subtract any element of that sum that represents payment for utilities that only benefited the tenant, for example gas, electricity and internet access. It is for the landlord to supply evidence of these, but if precise figures are not available an experienced tribunal will be able to make an informed estimate."*

It is helpful to put this part of the assessment in context.

In an earlier case, *Vadamalayan v Stewart and others* [2020] UKUT 183 (LC), the Upper Tribunal considered the context of the relevant HPA 2016 provisions relating to RROs. They are different substantially from the RRO provisions that were in the Housing Act 2004. Having considered both, it was held in *Vadamalayan* that expenditure by the landlord – such as mortgage payments or payments relating to the maintenance of the property – is not to be deducted (unlike what had occurred when considering the amount of RROs made pursuant to the relevant provisions of the 2004 Act).

At paragraph 15 of the *Vadamalayan* judgment Judge Elizabeth Cooke said the following when comparing the previous RRO provisions under the 2004 Act with those in the HPA 2016:

> "*That means that it is not appropriate to calculate a rent repayment order by deducting from the rent everything the landlord has spent on the property during the relevant period. That expenditure will have repaired or enhanced the landlord's own property, and will have enabled him to charge a rent for it. Much of the expenditure will have been incurred in meeting the landlord's obligations under the lease. The tenants will typically be entitled to have the structure of the property kept in repair and to have the property kept free of damp and pests. Often the tenancy will include a fridge, a cooker and so on. There is no reason why the landlord's costs in meeting his obligations under the lease should be set off against the cost of meeting his obligation to comply with a rent repayment order.*"

Returning then to the above example (maximum amount of £24,000), if we assume for these purposes that in each month of the 12-month relevant period within the payments made £90 was spent on utilities that only benefited the tenant(s), the figure in our example before moving on to step three would be £22,920 (£90 x 12 months = £1080; £24,000 - £1080 = £22,920).

Step Three: compare the offence

At this stage, the FTT should do two things with one central question being asked: how serious is this particular offence?

Firstly, it needs to consider how serious the offence that it has found the landlord to have committed was, both compared to other types of offence in respect of which an RRO may be made and compared to other examples of the same type of offence.

The first comparative exercise might, for example, on the facts of any given case lead to a view that failing to license an HMO or a house is not as severe as some of the other offences for which an RRO may be made. This was a point made by the Upper Tribunal in ***Hallet v. Parker*** [2022] UKUT 165 (LC)) by reference to the fact that s. 46 of the HPA 2016 does not include these 'licensing offences' within its ambit (see below for discussion of the more rigid approach to assessment within s. 46).

The FTT will then need to compare the offence before it to other examples of the same type of offence.

Secondly, it then needs to consider what proportion of the rent is a fair reflection of the seriousness of this offence.

These will be evaluative decisions for the FTT to make.

The figure that the FTT then has is taken as the starting point going into the final stage, which requires consideration of s. 44 (4) of the HPA 2016.

For the sake of illustration, we shall assume for the purposes of our example that having undertaken the assessment in line with this step the figure to be taken on to step four, below, is £15,000 – but this of course will be a highly fact-sensitive question the answer to which will differ case-by-case.

Step Four: consider deductions or additions in light of s. 44 (4) of the HPA 2016

To return to paragraph 20 of *Acheampong*, Judge Elizabeth Cooke said:

> *"d. Consider whether any deduction from, or addition to, that figure should be made in the light of the other factors set out in section 44(4)"*

Section 44 (4) of the HPA 2016 reads:

> *"(4) In determining the amount the tribunal must, in particular, take into account—*
>
> *(a) the conduct of the landlord and the tenant,*
>
> *(b) the financial circumstances of the landlord, and*
>
> *(c) whether the landlord has at any time been convicted of an offence to which this Chapter applies."*

All relevant circumstances may be considered, but the three listed from (a) to (c) must always be taken into account.

The "*...conduct of the landlord and the tenant...*" is broad and will change case by case, although the conduct must of course be relevant to the question being asked.

Failing to comply with the obligation to pay rent is relevant 'tenant conduct'.

As to (b) – the financial circumstances of the landlord – a landlord will want to produce documentary evidence so that the FTT can consider its relevance: savings, debts, income, employment, etc. A specialist tribunal such as the FTT should ask questions so as to obtain the necessary information (particularly if a party is not represented), but without documentary evidence corroborating what is said orally a tribunal may decide to place little weight on the answers provided in the hearing (an observation made by the Upper Tribunal in *Daff v. Gyalui* [2023] UKUT 134 (LC) at paragraph 27).

Finally the FTT must consider whether the landlord has at any time been convicted of an offence contained in the table in s. 40 (3) of the HPA 2016.

With the exception of this last point, consideration of the factors in s. 44 (4) of the HPA 2016 may lead to various allegations and counter-allegations.

In this respect, the Upper Tribunal has reminded the FTT that it need only consider all relevant circumstances and then arrive at a decision that falls within a reasonable range of responses open to it. In *Aytan v. Moore* [2022] UKUT 27 (LC) at paragraph 49 the Upper Tribunal (Judge Elizabeth Cooke and Judge Siobhan McGrath) said this:

> *"...we wish to make it clear that it is not appropriate for a tribunal to indulge in a fine-grained examination of every aspect of the parties' conduct, which would be disproportionate, nor in a detailed comparison of one landlord with another, which is unlikely to be accurate. The FTT must weigh the evidence and make a balanced decision. However, that exercise need not be a detailed forensic exercise as long as all relevant circumstances are taken into account and the outcome falls within the reasonable range of responses available to the Tribunal."*

Returning to our example, it will be recalled that the figure at this stage is £15,000. This fourth step would require the FTT to consider the factors in s. 44 (4) of the HPA 2016 and decide, having done so, whether any additions to or deductions from that £15,000 were merited.

Having done this, the figure then arrived at is the amount of the RRO.

Below is a summary of a number of appeals illustrating how certain factors have influenced the assessment of an RRO award, but they should be considered as illustrations only; the amount of an RRO in any given case will always be a matter for the evaluative judgment of the FTT having considered the particulars facts of the case before it. Because of this, the Upper Tribunal will only allow an appeal against the amount ordered by the FTT if it had misdirected itself in law or had failed to take a relevant matter into account when making the assessment.

Examples of RRO awards

In *Williams v. Parmar* [2021] UKUT 244 (LC) a landlord had failed to obtain a licence in respect of an HMO that required one. The condition of the property was such that without further substantial works an HMO licence would not have been granted. She was a professional landlord (although see below on the use of such a label) with no relevant convictions. The deficiencies in the property were serious and affected the comfort of all the tenants (with one tenant's room being particularly affected). An 80% RRO was awarded (90% in the case of the tenant whose room was particularly impacted).

Aytan v. Moore [2022] UKUT 27 (LC) involved two appeals heard together.

In one, the conduct of the tenants and condition of the property was of no material relevance to the RRO amount nor were arguments advanced regarding the landlord's financial circumstances or relevant convictions. The main issue was that the landlord did not have a licence of the property despite owning nine flats in the building in which the premises in question were situated, plus having extensive commercial property interests and company directorships. They were seen as "*...serious property investors...*" (paragraph 51 of the judgment), but there was no evidence of harm to the tenants as a result of the offence. The Upper Tribunal substituted the FTT's order with an 85% RRO.

In the other appeal (*Wilson v. Arrow & Others* [2022] UKUT 27 (LC), also involving the offence of being in control of or managing an unlicensed HMO, the property in question was not immediately eligible for a licence because it required the fitting of fire doors and alarms. There was no evidence relating to the landlord's financial circumstances or previous convictions. The fire-safety defects (not remedied for over 12 months) were described by the Upper Tribunal as a very serious matter and it awarded the tenants 90% of the maximum amount.

In *Simpson House 3 Ltd v Osserman* [2022] UKUT 164 (LC) the FTT had awarded an RRO against the landlord, a substantial property investment company in control of or managing an unlicensed HMO, representing 65% of the rent, but the Upper Tribunal upon appeal by the tenants set this aside and made a higher RRO representing 80% of the rent. An important factor was that the landlord had served notices to terminate the tenancy in response to complaints about the need for repairs. The landlord was further criticised for misrepresenting the consequences for the tenants of not vacating by the date stated in the s.21 Housing Act 1988 notice (it having been suggested to them that they risked forfeiting their deposit or adverse credit scores as a result).

In *Hallett v Parker* [2022] UKUT 165 (LC) the (unlicensed) property had originally been the landlord's home but had for some time been let via an agent. It was the landlord's only property let out and it was the first occasion it had been let to a group of tenants not forming a single household – and therefore the first time a licence was required. The condition of the property was said to be fairly good and the landlord applied for and was granted a licence as soon as he became aware of the need. The Upper Tribunal also took account of the fact that his agents had not alerted him about the need to get a licence when he might reasonably have expected them to. The Upper Tribunal set aside the award of the FTT and ordered repayment of 25% of the rent. It was also said at paragraph 30 of the judgment that where s.46 of the HPA 2016 is not engaged (see below for a discussion of this provision) requiring repayment of the full amount of the rent received by a landlord should be reserved for the most serious offences, and the Upper Tribunal also accepted that an absence of convictions for other housing offences was a relevant consideration in a landlord's favour. In contrast, not receiving a financial penalty from an LHA for the offence was not (paragraph 35 of the judgment).

In *Kowalek v Hassanein Ltd* [2022] EWCA Civ 1041 a 50% reduction was awarded by the FTT due to significant rent arrears (appeals to the Upper Tribunal and Court of Appeal did not impact the amount of the RRO). The Court of Appeal rejected an argument that a tenant's failure to pay rent was not capable of being an aspect of their conduct which it was proper to take into account when determining the amount of an RRO (the unsuccessful argument being that the non-payment of rent was already factored into the RRO because of s.44 (2) of the HPA 2016).

In *Hancher v David and others* [2022] UKUT 277 (LC), 65% of the rent was ordered to be repaid. The landlord had been in control of or managing an HMO that required a licence but did not have one, but the Upper Tribunal found that this offence was not one of the more serious offences for which an RRO can be made nor was the offence in question one of the more serious of its type (see paragraph 19 of the judgment). Further, although some improvements were needed at the property there was no evidence of fire hazards and no suggestion that the property would not have qualified for an HMO licence had one been sought. However, the landlord had been on notice of the need to the obtain a licence and had deliberately failed to get one.

In *Dowd v. Martins* [2022] UKUT 249 (LC) the landlord was managing an unlicensed HMO, it being accepted that this was because the landlord did not know one was needed, but he had waited three months from finding out about the need to apply for one. *Hallett* (above) was invoked as a comparator on behalf of the landlord, but the Upper Tribunal was of the view that the offence was significantly more serious than in that case and made an RRO representing 45% of the rent.

In one of the appeals heard in *Acheampong v. Roman* [2022] UKUT 239 (LC) the Upper Tribunal substituted a figure of 75% of the maximum rent. The landlord, a Mr Choudhury, admitted being in control of or managing a house which required a licence but did not have one. The maximum rent for the purposes of step one was £18,000. The property was said not to be in a satisfactory condition because of some damp and mould, the tenancy deposit was not protected, the landlord did not hold gas or fire safety certificates and there were failings in fire safety equipment (the fire safety failings and deposit protection breaches being described by the Upper Tribunal as 'significant'). However, the offence was not the most serious of its kind. Consideration of the three factors in s. 44 (4) of the HPA 2016 did not lead to any change and an RRO relating to 75% of the maximum rent was made.

In *Daff v Gyalui* [2023] UKUT 134 (LC), the property was subject to a selective licensing scheme but the landlord had no licence, saying she did not know of the need for one. She had provided information to the FTT addressing her financial circumstances, such as her expenditure – including on a mortgage and service charges – totalling £24,409 as well as living expenses and the cost of medicines and medical treatment (the landlord was said to have a serious debilitating illness). This financial information, however, had not been considered by the FTT, which was an error. Comparatively the offence was not severe, both in terms of the other offences for which an RRO can be made and other licensing offences (stage three of *Acheampong*), but it was an offence and she had failed to take steps to inform herself of her obligations. She had spent time living abroad (Australia) and was abroad when the licensing scheme was introduced, and her agent had not advised her of its introduction. In substituting an RRO in the sum of £2000, the Upper Tribunal said the circumstances of the case were exceptional: limited means, very poor health contributing to her lack of attentiveness and generally she was in a precarious financial position. The Upper Tribunal also suggested that the FTT should resist the temptation to classify a landlord as 'professional' or 'amateur' as a more nuanced analysis will often be required.

In *Newell v. Abbott* [2024] UKUT 181 (LC) the landlord was in control of or managed an unlicensed house. The Upper Tribunal reviewed some recent decisions it had given dealing with the amount of RROs and observed that factors which have tended to result in higher penalties include that the offence was committed deliberately or by a commercial landlord or an individual with a larger property portfolio or where tenants have been exposed to poor or dangerous conditions which have been prolonged due to the failure to obtain a licence. Conversely, factors tending to lead to lower penalties included inadvertence on the part of a smaller landlord, property that was in good condition and mitigating factors which go some way to explain (but not excuse) the offence (see paragraph 57 of the judgment). Having applied this to the facts, a 60% RRO was made.

The amount of a rent repayment order where the application is made by a local housing authority (s. 45 of the HPA 2016)

Local housing authorities ("LHA") may apply for an RRO, but in respect of a relevant award of universal credit paid to any person in respect of rent under the tenancy.

Save for the references to 'rent' and 'universal credit', as may be expected, the approach to be taken to determining the amount of an RRO where the applicant is a tenant and where it is an LHA is similar. The relevant statutory provisions are very similar (s. 44 of the HPA 2016 in respect of applications by tenant(s) and s. 45, LHAs).

Having said this, the vast majority of the appeals to the Upper Tribunal relating to RROs have involved tenants rather than LHAs and practitioners dealing with applications by LHAs for the repayment of universal credit should consider, in particular, sections 43 & 45 of the HPA 2016.

These provisions are the focus of the following section.

The approach

As is the case with tenants, an LHA may apply to the FTT for an RRO against a person who has committed an offence contained in s. 40 (3) of the HPA 2016 (s. 41 (1)) and for these purposes it will be recalled that an RRO is an order requiring the landlord under a tenancy of housing in England to (a) repay an amount of rent paid by a tenant *or* (b) pay an

LHA an amount in respect of a relevant award of universal credit paid (to any person) in respect of rent under the tenancy. (s. 40 (2) of the HPA 2016).

An LHA may only apply for an RRO if the offence relates to housing in its area (s. 41 (3) (a) of the HPA 2016).

When an LHA applies for an RRO s.42 of the HPA 2016 requires it to take an additional step to the steps to be taken by tenants. This relates to it having to give to the landlord a notice stating that it is intending to apply for an RRO.

This process is addressed in Chapter 5, which deals with the procedure relating to applications for RROs. What follows deals with how the FTT should approach quantification of an RRO made in favour of an LHA.

The amount of such an order is to be determined in accordance with section 45 of the HPA 2016 (see also s. 43 (3) (b) of the HPA 2016).

Section 45 is entitled *"Amount of order: local housing authorities"*. It confirms that the amount of the RRO must relate to universal credit paid during the period mentioned in the following table:

In the order is made on the ground that the landlord has committed	*the amount must relate to universal credit paid in respect of*
an offence mentioned in row 1 or 2 of the table in section 40(3)	the period of 12 months ending with the date of the offence
an offence mentioned in row 3, 4, 5, 6 or 7 of the table in section 40(3)	a period, not exceeding 12 months, during which the landlord was committing the offence

This table is in all material respects the same as the table included above and found in s. 44 (2) of the HPA 2016 relevant to applications made by tenants, save for the necessary substitution of 'the amount must relate to universal credit paid in respect of' instead of 'the amount must relate to rent by paid by the tenant in respect of'.

The maximum amount that the landlord may be required to repay to the LHA must not exceed the amount of universal credit they – the landlord – received directly or indirectly in respect of rent under the tenancy for the period referred to in table (see s. 45 (3) of the HPA 2016).

The words 'directly or indirectly' in relation to the sums being received make it clear that it does not matter if the particular payment was passed on to the landlord by, for example, the tenant or received directly from the LHA – or a different person or body. The qualifying condition is simply that the landlord must have received it and that it was in respect of rent under the tenancy for the appropriate period.

References in Part 2, Chapter 4, of the HPA 2016 to 'universal credit' or to a 'relevant award of universal credit' include 'housing benefit', and where an LHA applies for an RRO in relation to housing benefit references to 'rent' includes any payment in respect of which housing benefit may be paid. See sections 51 and 52 of the HPA 2016.

Finally, the FTT when determining the amount must, in particular, take into account the following three factors: the conduct of the landlord, the financial circumstances of the landlord and whether the landlord has at any time been convicted of an offence to which this chapter applies (see s.45 (4) of the HPA 2016).

With one exception, these three factors are identical to the three factors that must be considered by the FTT when determining the amount of an RRO in favour of a tenant. The difference is that in determining the amount of an RRO in favour of an LHA the FTT is not expressly required to take account of the conduct of the tenant, which may be seen as a logical omission considering the nature and purpose of RROs in favour of an LHA.

The approach to determining the amount of an RRO where a landlord has previous convictions (s.46 of the HPA 2016)

Section 46 of the HPA 2016 has been referred to above because, when it is engaged, it requires a different approach to the determination by the FTT of the amount of an RRO (see s.44 (3) (c)).

As explained fully below s.46 will apply where the landlord has been convicted or received a financial penalty in respect of the offence.

Starting with s.44 (3) (c):

> *"(3) The amount of a rent repayment order under this section is to be determined in accordance with—*
>
> *(a)...*
>
> *(b)...*
>
> *(c) section 46 (in certain cases where the landlord has been convicted etc)."*

Section 46 of the HPA 2016 is entitled *"Amount of order following conviction"*.

Where it applies, the amount of the RRO is to be the maximum that the FTT has power to order in accordance with section 44 or 45. Furthermore, it expressly disregards from that consideration – the question of amount – the criteria contained in s. 44 (4) (RROs made in favour of tenants) and s. 45 (4) (RROs made in favour of an LHA).

In other words, where section 46 of the HPA 2016 applies the FTT shall order the maximum to be repaid and it may not have regard to the conduct of the landlord or tenant, the financial circumstances of the landlord or whether the landlord has at any time been convicted of an offence to which Chapter 4 of Part 2 of the 2016 Act applies (because the amount of the RRO will be the maximum that the FTT has power to award), although this is subject to a discretion to order less as a result of 'exceptional circumstances' (discussed below).

The maximum amount will therefore be determined in the same way: by following sections 44 and 45 for tenants and LHAs, respectively.

When will section 46 HPA 2016 apply?

Subject to exceptional circumstances, the amount of an RRO will be the maximum permitted where:

(1) firstly, as in all cases, the FTT decides to make an RRO under s.43 HPA 2016. This is of course a pre-condition for the making of an RRO and requires the FTT to be satisfied, beyond reasonable doubt, that a landlord has committed an offence to which Chapter 4, Part 2 applies, whether or not the landlord has been convicted; and

(2) secondly either:

    a. the RRO is made against a landlord who has been convicted of the offence. It will be noted that the requirement here is that the landlord *has been convicted* (rather than *has committed*); or

    b. the RRO is made against a landlord who has received a financial penalty in respect of the offence and is made at a time when there is no prospect of appeal against that penalty;

    (this is referred to as 'Condition 1');

    and

(3) thirdly either:

a. the order is made in favour of a tenant on the ground that the landlord has committed an offence mentioned in row 1, 2, 3, 4 or 7 of the table in section 40(3); or

b. The order is made in favour of an LHA.

(this is referred to as 'Condition 2').

It will be noted in respect of Condition 2 that the offences mentioned in rows 5 and 6 are missing from those listed and that those two offences are the 'licensing offences' contained in s. 72 (1) and 95 (1), respectively, of the Housing Act 2004. See the end of this chapter in respect of proposals to change this.

By s. 56 of the HPA 2016 a financial penalty as referred to in Condition 1 means a penalty that is imposed in respect of conduct that amounts to an offence, but is imposed otherwise than following the person's conviction for the offence. There will be *"no prospect of appeal"* in relation to such a penalty when the period for appealing it has expired and any appeal has been finally determined or withdrawn (s. 46 (4) of the HPA 2016).

By virtue of s. 46 (5) of the HPA 2016 if by reason of exceptional circumstances the FTT considers it would be unreasonable to require the landlord to pay an amount then that amount may be removed from the RRO award.

Whether circumstances are "exceptional" or not so as to make it unreasonable for the landlord to have to pay some or all of the amount is a matter for the judgment of the FTT, which means the conclusion reached after such an assessment would be difficult to appeal: it will have to be established that the FTT had misdirected itself in law or had failed to take a relevant matter into account when undertaking the assessment.

A good example of this is the case of *Ball v. Sefton Metropolitan Borough Council* [2021] UKUT 42 (LC) where the landlord had been convicted at the Magistrates Court following a guilty plea of having control of an unlicensed HMO, and thereafter the Borough Council applied to the FTT seeking back all the sums it had paid to the landlord in universal credit.

The landlord had received £10 per day for each tenant and out of that had to meet running costs, including interest payments on a loan used to purchase the property. The operation of the HMO was loss-making. The FTT, however, made an RRO in favour of the Borough Council against the landlord in respect of the full amount received. Despite the financial position, the Upper Tribunal on appeal would not change the order. It was satisfied that it was open to the FTT to have determined that the circumstances were not such as to amount to 'exceptional circumstances' as required by s. 46 (5) of the HPA 2016.

Changes proposed by the Renters' Rights Bill

The Renters' Rights Bill 2024-25 will, as drafted at the time of writing, result in important changes to matters relevant to the determination of the amount of an RRO.

What follows is a summary of the likely changes but as the Bill may change before it is passed it is important that practitioners ensure that they are referring to the latest version of the HPA 2016 subject to any applicable amendments.

Increasing the 'relevant period' to two years: the period to which the maximum amount of an RRO must relate is to be increased from 12 months to two years. This is proposed to apply to both applications made by tenants and LHAs.

Rent paid before (or after) the offence: the Bill proposes to remove one of the effects of the Court of Appeal's decision in *Kowalek* discussed above. The change would remove the current requirement reiterated in that decision that the amount of the RRO must relate to rent paid *during* the period as well as in respect of that period (the latter requirement only remaining). The proposed change would mean, for example, that rent paid in advance at a time when there was no offence being committed (e.g consider the licensing offence in s. 72 (1) Housing Act 2004 before a property is occupied) then as long as the rent was paid in respect of a period when the licensing offence was committed the amount in question could form part of the RRO. Again, this is proposed to apply to both applications made by tenants and LHAs.

Broadening the scope of Section 46 of the HPA 2016: the Bill will also likely change the current requirement contained in s. 46 (1) of the HPA 2016 that *both* conditions within it (referred to as Condition 1 and Condition 2) be satisfied and, instead, the Bill is likely to allow the maximum RRO to be awarded in the circumstances mentioned if *either* of them is.

The Bill further proposes to broaden the scope of 'Condition 2' within s. 46 of the HPA 2016 in two ways.

The first relates to the offences that may trigger the maximum award. Currently an RRO made in favour of a tenant will not come within the scope of s.46 of the HPA 2016 if the offence that is committed is either of the two licensing offences (s. 72 (1) & s. 95 (1) of the Housing Act 2004). This is because s. 46 (3) (a) of the HPA 2016 currently does not refer to the two licensing offences that appear in rows 5 and 6 of the table in s.40 (3). The proposed change would add these two licensing offences.

The second proposed change to s. 46 (3) of the HPA 2016 would further broaden its application in that it would apply to landlords who at any time have (a) been convicted of another offence which is the same offence as the offence under consideration (b) received a financial penalty in respect of another offence which is the same as that offence under consideration or (c) had an RRO made against them in respect of another offence which is the same offence as the one under consideration. This would be so whether or not the other offence, financial penalty or RRO (as the case may be) was in relation to the same tenancy or housing as the one being considered.

Other likely changes: when determining the amount of an RRO the FTT is likely to be required to consider, in particular, not just the three factors currently in s. 44 (4) (RROs in favour of a tenant) and s. 45 (4) (RROs in favour of an LHA) but also whether or not the landlord has received a financial penalty and whether they have at any time had an RRO made against them.

Summary

- The approach to determining the amount of an RRO will depend upon whether it is an order in favour of a tenant, an LHA or where the landlord has been convicted of the offence or received a financial penalty in respect of it;
- In recent years the Upper Tribunal and the Courts have on many occasions interpreted the provisions applicable to determining the amount of an RRO made in favour of a tenant and a methodical approach to that assessment has developed, although the amount will always be the product of a fact-specific analysis;
- Looking ahead the (likely) amendments to be brought about by the Renters' Rights Bill are all intended to further deter rogue landlords and further pressure landlords to comply with, e.g, certain housing standards: increasing the potential size of the awards, allowing rent paid in advance to qualify and expanding the situations in which the maximum amount can be made (for example).

CHAPTER FIVE

THE PROCEDURE RELATING TO RENT REPAYMENT ORDERS

Introduction

The focus of this chapter is on procedure: how is an RRO sought and how will the First-tier Tribunal (Property Chamber) ("the FTT") deal with the application?

Are there time limits in which applications for RRO must be brought?

What can be done if a party wants to challenge the outcome?

When, if ever, can one party claim their legal costs from another?

With its focus on procedure the chapter also covers an important additional step that Local Housing Authorities ("LHAs") – unlike tenants – must take before they can apply for an RRO.

Making an Application for a Rent Repayment Order

The application form & fees

In respect of applications for a rent repayment order ("RRO") the form to be used is form RRO1, which is available publicly on the gov.uk website.[2] It is to be used by both tenants and LHAs when applying to the FTT for an RRO.

An applicant starts proceedings before the FTT by sending or delivering to it a notice of application: see rule 26 (1) of the *Tribunal Procedure (First-tier Tribunal) (Property Chamber) Rules* 2013 ("the FTT's Procedural Rules"). Rule 26 of the FTT's Procedural Rules should be considered in full when submitting an application using RRO1: it contains a long list of information and documentation to be included and other requirements, including that the application be signed, dated and accompanied by the appropriate fee.

If an applicant starts proceedings before the FTT by sending or delivering to it a notice of application, what if the appropriate fee is not paid or tendered when sending or delivering that application? Have the proceedings 'started'?

This is important because by s. 41 (2) (b) of the Housing and Planning Act 2016 ("the HPA 2016") a tenant may apply for an RRO only if the offence was committed in the period of 12 months ending with the day on which the application is made. Is the application 'made' for these purposes if it was not accompanied by the fee or a tendering of the fee?

In the Upper Tribunal (Lands Chamber) ("the Upper Tribunal") decision of *Jevan v Athansiadi* [2024] UKUT 358 (LC) it was decided that the effective commencement of FTT proceedings did not require that the appropriate fee first be paid or tendered. Rule 26 (5) of the FTT's Procedural Rules says that an applicant must 'provide' with the notice of application any fee payable to it, but that read both alone and alongside other rules did not mean that the proceedings had not 'started'. It was decided that proceedings are started by sending or delivering a notice of

2 See RRO1 "*Application by Tenant or Local Housing Authority for a Rent Repayment Order*"

application to the FTT, whether or not the requisite fee is paid at the same time.

As well as providing the parties' details and information relating to the property to which the RRO application relates, the RRO1 form requires an applicant to state the grounds for making the application and to give details of the amount sought. If the applicant is a tenant, this requires enclosing evidence that rent has been paid in respect of occupation of the premises during the period in which it is alleged that the offence has been committed.

Currently there is a £110 application fee to be paid when making the RRO application (Schedule 1 of the *First-tier Tribunal (Property Chamber) Fees Order* 2013/1179 (as amended)). An applicant may, however, consider making an application for Help with Fees using Form EX160, which can be read alongside guidance contained in form EX160A.

Pursuant to rule 11 of the FTT's Procedural Rules the FTT must not proceed further with the RRO application until the fee is paid. Where a fee remains unpaid for a period of 14 days after the date on which the fee is payable the case, if not already started, must not be started. Similarly, where the case has started, it shall be deemed to be withdrawn 14 days after the date on which the FTT sends or delivers to the party liable to make payment a written notification that the fee has not been paid.

Where the applicant is an LHA evidence should be enclosed with the application of universal credit or housing benefit having been paid for rent in respect of occupation of the premises during the period in which it is alleged that an offence has been committed, along with a copy of the notice of intended proceedings required under s.42 of the HPA 2016 (see further below in respect of these notices).

The RRO1 form also has a section where the applicant may state that they would be content for the application to be determined without a hearing (known as a paper determination). This, however, will not be granted unless the FTT thinks such a procedure is appropriate and unless the parties and others have been notified of their right to attend a hearing and consent to the hearing being determined based upon written submissions. Any party that wants a hearing may request one.

A further fee will be payable by the applicant upon receiving the notice of the hearing date (if the FTT lists the application for a hearing). Currently, this hearing fee is £220 (again, see Schedule 1 of the *First-tier Tribunal (Property Chamber) Fees Order* 2013/1179 (as amended)).

Time limits for making an application for an RRO

There is a time limit imposed upon applicants after which an application for an RRO may not be brought; if the application is brought out of time, it will be dismissed on the basis that FTT has no power to make the order.

This time limit is imposed by s. 41 (2) of the HPA 2016, which states that a tenant may apply for an RRO only if:

(a) the offence relates to housing that, at the time of the offence, was let to the tenant; and

(b) the offence was committed in the period of 12 months ending with the day on which the application is made.

(note, however, the end of this chapter regarding proposals to increase this period from 12 months to two years).

This time limit is not capable of being extended by the FTT. In *Gurusinghe v Drumlin Ltd* [2021] UKUT 268 (LC) an application had been made for an RRO wherein it was alleged that the landlord was guilty of the offence of managing or controlling an unlicensed HMO as contained in s. 72 (1) of the Housing Act 2004. Later, the applicant tenants wanted to substitute or add to the respondents named on the RRO application form for another entity on the basis that the named respondents might not have been the correct landlord. The FTT, however, refused the application.

On appeal the Upper Tribunal agreed with the FTT: as the 12-month limit contained in s. 42 (1) (b) of the HPA 2016 had expired there was no power to add or substitute the respondent. The application to add or substitute the named respondents was made more than 12 months after the offence was committed.

In *Tze Moh v. Rimal Properties Ltd* [2024] UKUT 324 (LC) the Upper Tribunal (Judge Eliabeth Cooke) identified the following two questions in respect of two separate appeals, each of which related to the 12-month period contained in s.42 (1) (b) and the offence of being in control of or managing an unlicensed HMO in s. 72 (1) of the Housing Act 2004:

(1) how long does a tenant have to make an application for an RRO against a landlord who has been managing an HMO without a licence after they have acquired a defence to the offence created by section 72(1) of the Housing Act 2004?

(2) what is meant in s. 41 (2) (b) of the HPA 2016 by the words "*... the period of 12 months ending with the day on which the application is made.*"?

The facts of both applications are worth setting out in detail.

In one case the landlord had on 4th May 2022 applied for an HMO licence at 13:44hrs; the tenant applicants had made their application for an RRO to the FTT on 4th May 2023 at 15:36hrs. The FTT had held that the last day on which an offence had been committed was 3rd May 2022 thereby excluding the day on which the application for an HMO licence was made. It further held that the "*period of 12 months ending with the day on which the application is made*" as contained in s. 41 (2) (b) of the HPA 2016 began at the first moment of 5 May 2022.

In the other application the landlord had sought to apply for an HMO licence on 16th November 2022 but was unable to pay the fee because the LHA's website was not functioning. At 16:00hrs on the same day the landlord emailed the LHA to alert it to the problem, and received a response at 18:02hrs explaining that the payment system was down and promising to tell him when the problem was resolved. The licence fee was paid in December once the problem was resolved. The FTT had held that the last date on which the landlord had committed the offence was 15th November 2022 and that the landlord had the defence of reasonable excuse contained in s. 72 (5) of the Housing Act 2004 from 16th November 2022 onwards. As the RRO application to the FTT was made on 15th November 2023 the FTT held that it was made out of time.

In its decision the Upper Tribunal noted that s. 41 (2) (b) does not talk of a period of 12 months "*before*" the application to the FTT or a period "*after*" the last day on which the offence was committed:

> "*A period of 12 months ending on a particular date is not the same – as a matter of ordinary language – as the period of 12 months before that date. The language implies that the start and end date are each within the period.*" (paragraph 38)

Applying this to the first case it was held that the period is one of 12 months, meaning it started on 5th May 2022 and ended with the date on which the RRO application was made, which was the 4th May 2023.

In respect of the other question that had to be answered – the date on which the defence took effect – it was held that for reasons of simplicity fractions of days did not count. Further, because of the possibility of criminal liability any ambiguity in this respect ought to be resolved in favour of the landlord.

Put differently, it was held that it was preferable to say that a landlord had a defence in the morning because he applied for a licence later in the day, rather than to say that he was committing an offence all afternoon and evening even though he had already applied for a licence.

Both applications for RROs were therefore out of time.

The "notice of intended proceedings": applications made by Local Housing Authorities

By s. 42 (1) of the HPA 2016 there is an additional procedural step imposed upon an LHA that it must take before it makes its application for an RRO.

This stage involves the LHA providing the landlord with what s.42 of the HPA 2016 refers to as a 'notice of intended proceedings'.

In summary the following will apply to an LHA:

- Because of s. 41 (3) of the HPA 2016 an LHA may not make an application for an RRO unless the offence relates to housing in the authority's area and the LHA has complied with section 42;

- Compliance with s.42 of the HPA 2016 requires the LHA to give to the landlord the aforementioned notice of intended proceedings (see s. 42 (1));

- Such a notice given by the LHA must:

    - Inform the landlord that the authority is proposing to apply for an RRO and explain why;

    - state the amount that the authority seeks to recover; and

    - invite the landlord to make representations within a period specified in the notice of not less than 28 days (which is referred to as "the notice period").

- The authority must then consider any representations made during the notice period (s.42 (3) of the HPA 2016) and may not apply for an RRO before the notice period has ended (s.42 (4) of the HPA 2016).

A further important restriction is imposed upon an LHA by virtue of the fact that a notice of intended proceedings may not be given after the end of the period of 12 months beginning with the day on which the landlord committed the offence to which it relates (s. 42 (5) of the HPA 2016).

This serves the same purpose as the time limit in s. 41 (2) (b) in respect of applications made by tenants.

LHAs also have a 'duty to consider applying' for an RRO in circumstances where it becomes aware that a person has been convicted of an offence to which Chapter 4 applies in relation to housing in its area (s.48 of the HPA 2016).

Furthermore by s. 41 (4) of the HPA 2016 in deciding whether to apply for an RRO an LHA must have regard to any guidance given by the Secretary of State, and guidance has been issued by the Department for Communities and Local Government entitled "*Rent repayment orders under the Housing and Planning Act 2016: Guidance for Local Housing Authorities*".

A copy of it is available publicly on the gov.uk website.

The requirement to give the landlord a notice of intended proceedings applies only to LHAs.

Case management at the FTT & the hearing of the application for an RRO

If the FTT is satisfied that the application for an RRO has been properly made, including payment of or exemption from any fee, a copy of the application and any supporting documents will be sent to the respondent(s).

Unless the FTT has directed otherwise, the respondent must within 28 days after the date on which it was provided with a copy of the notice of application send or deliver to the FTT its response, and at the same time send a copy of the response and any accompanying documents to the applicant and any other parties.

Rule 30 of the FTT's Procedural Rules contains specific information in respect of what the response must contain.

Written directions tend to be sent to the parties following consideration by a judge of the application and will often identity in writing what the issues for determination appear to be, as well as summarising the amount that it is sought by the applicant and the period in respect of which the particular offence is said to relate. There may also be directions for further evidence and provision of documentation on which a party may wish to rely, as well as directing who shall produce the hearing bundle.

The time, date and location of the hearing will be provided along with the estimated length of the hearing itself. The hearing length obviously depends upon the issues that need to be determined in any given case, but hearings to determine applications for RROs tend to be listed for between half a day and a day.

The hearing

Where there is a hearing, a fee will become payable by the applicant when they receive notice of the date from the FTT (see above).

Reasonable notice of the hearing – and any adjourned or postponed hearing – must be given to each party. Save where the circumstances are felt to be urgent or exceptional – unlikely to apply in an application for an RRO – or where the parties consent, the notice of the final hearing that will dispose of the application must be no less than 14 days (rule 32 of the FTT's Procedural Rules).

As for the hearing itself because applications for RROs will inevitably involve disputes of fact or opinion it is usually heard by two members of the FTT, one of whom is likely to be a lawyer or surveyor. It is that person that has responsibility for the conduct of the case and produces the written reasons for the decision.

By rule 34 of the FTT's Procedural Rules the FTT may proceed with a hearing in the absence of a party if:

(a) It is satisfied that the party has been notified of the hearing or that reasonable steps have been taken to notify the party of the hearing; and

(b) considers that it is in the interests of justice to proceed with the hearing.

Although the conduct of the hearing will always be controlled by the Judge, hearings of RRO applications often begin with the applicant giving their evidence first and the respondent being permitted to ask them questions, with the roles then reversed. The FTT will have directed which party is to produce and provide copies of the hearing bundle, and this bundle will be (or should be) available for the witnesses and is likely to be referred to extensively by all parties and the FTT throughout.

Once the evidence is heard the parties will then usually be asked to make their closing representations. Thereafter, although the FTT may give its decision orally (see rule 36 (1) of the FTT's Procedural Rules), the decision is often reserved to a later date. In any event, as the hearing in question will be one finally disposing of all issues the FTT must provide each party with a written decision containing a notice of the decision and reasons for it along with notification of any right of appeal and the time within which, and manner in which, such right of appeal may be exercised (see rule 36 (2) of the FTT's Procedural Rules).

There is an extensive public database of RRO decisions made by the FTT that is available on the gov.uk website (see its 'residential property tribunal decisions' section).

Challenging RROs: reviews and appeals

General

Any party has a right to appeal to the Upper Tribunal on "any point of law" arising from a decision made by the FTT, but importantly that right is subject to first getting permission either from the FTT or from the Upper Tribunal. This will require a party to make an application seeking permission (s.11 (1) to (4) of the Tribunals, Courts and Enforcement Act 2007).

Seeking permission to appeal from the FTT

A party must first seek permission to appeal from the FTT before applying to the Upper Tribunal. See rule 21 (2) of the *Tribunal Procedure (Upper Tribunal) (Lands Chamber)* Rules 2010/2600 ("the Upper Tribunal's Procedural Rules"). In respect of seeking permission to appeal from the FTT a party should use Form RP PTA, again available publicly via the gov.uk website under the 'Courts, Sentencing and Tribunals' section.

A party has 28 days to send their written application from the date that the FTT sends to them its written reasons for the decision, although the FTT does have a power to extend that time (see rule 52 (1) to (4) of the FTT's Procedural Rules). If the implementation of the RRO is something that the party seeking permission to appeal wishes to have stayed pending the outcome of the appeal this must be sought at the same time (rule 54 of the FTT's Procedural Rules).

In this respect it should be noted that an amount payable under an RRO is recoverable as a debt (s. 47 (1) of the HPA 2016).

Upon receipt of an application for permission to appeal the FTT must first consider whether to review the decision. One advantage of such a procedure – permitting a review of the decision upon receipt of an application for permission to appeal it – is that it may prevent matters unnecessarily going to the Upper Tribunal. However, the FTT should make it clear which parts of a decision it intends to review and, if so satisfied, which parts of it it intends to set aside.

The review process is not, therefore, a reassessment of the entire case or an opportunity for the parties to put forward new arguments.

The FTT may only undertake a review of a decision if it is satisfied that a ground of appeal is likely to be successful (rule 55 (1) of the FTT's Procedural Rules). The primary purpose of the power to review its decision is to avoid an unnecessary appeal to the Upper Tribunal where the FTT has made an obvious error of law (*Point West GR Ltd v. Bassi* [2020] EWCA Civ 795).

If the FTT decides not to review the decision, or reviews it but decides to take no action, it must then by virtue of rule 53 of the FTT's Procedural Rules consider whether to give permission to appeal. Having done this, the FTT will then send a record of its decision to the parties as soon as practicable.

If the FTT refuses permission to appeal the record will contain a statement of its reasons for such refusal along with a notification of the right to make an application to the Upper Tribunal for permission to appeal, including the time within which, and the method by which, such application must be made (rule 53 (3) & (4) of the FTT's Procedural Rules).

If, however, permission to appeal to the Upper Tribunal is given by the FTT then the appellant has one month to provide the Upper Tribunal with their notice of appeal (see rule 24 of the Upper Tribunal's Procedural Rules in relation to the time limit and what the appellant is required to do at this stage).

Seeking permission to appeal from the Upper Tribunal

If the FTT refused the application, permission to appeal may be sought from the Upper Tribunal. This application must be made in writing and received by the Upper Tribunal no later than 14 days after the date on which the FTT sent notice of its refusal of permission to appeal (or sent notice that permission was granted but only on limited grounds, as the case may be).

The application for permission to appeal to the Upper Tribunal should be made using Form T602, and practitioners should refer to rule 21 of the Upper Tribunal's Procedural Rules as it contains detailed information as to what is required at this stage.

The Upper Tribunal will send a copy of the application for permission to appeal and its supporting documents to the respondent and give a time limit within which any representations the respondent wishes to make must be made (unless the Upper Tribunal simply decides to dismiss the application without such representations) (rule 21 (8) of the Upper Tribunal's Procedural Rules). It is at this stage open to the respondent to include an application for permission to cross-appeal – including the grounds – if the appellant's application is granted. In respect of RROs this could, for example, see a landlord cross-appeal on the basis that a defence had been wrongly rejected or that the RRO was too high – in contrast to the tenant's arguments that, for example, the RRO amount was too low.

If the Upper Tribunal refuses permission to appeal it will send the applicant a written notice along with the reasons for its refusal. By s.13 (1) & (8) (c) of the Tribunals, Courts and Enforcement Act 2007 there is no right of appeal to the Court of Appeal against a decision of the Upper Tribunal to refuse permission to appeal, but in very limited circumstances an applicant may apply for judicial review of the decision (see r.54.7A of the Civil Procedure Rules).

If, however, permission to appeal is granted by the Upper Tribunal then unless directed otherwise the application for permission to appeal will be treated as the notice of appeal, and Part 4 of the Upper Tribunal's Procedural Rules contains the provisions that relate to notices from respondents and appellants' replies.

In terms of the hearing before the Upper Tribunal if it does find that there was an error by the FTT on a point of law it may (but does not have to) set aside the decision and, if it does, it must either remit the matter back to the FTT (usually in front of a different panel) or remake the decision.

As discussed in Chapter 4 regarding the approach to the determination of RROs it is not uncommon for the Upper Tribunal, if it feels the appropriate findings of fact have been made, to substitute an RRO award made by the FTT with its own (meaning a lower or higher award).

Appeals from decisions of the Upper Tribunal

Practitioners considering seeking permission to appeal a decision of the Upper Tribunal (not including a decision to refuse permission to appeal to it, which is discussed above), should refer to the rules in Part 11 of the Upper Tribunal's Procedural Rules, in particular rule 55.

If an application to the Upper Tribunal for permission to appeal its decision is refused by it, an application seeking permission may be made to the Court of Appeal. Such an application can only be made if the Upper Tribunal has first refused an application for permission to appeal its decision (s.13 of the Tribunals, Courts and Enforcement Act 2007).

Finally, it should be noted that there is a separate provision in s. 53 (1) of the HPA 2016 giving a right to appeal RRO decisions made by the FTT to the Upper Tribunal. The circumstances, however, are limited and in any event the right is once again subject to a requirement that permission is first given. It will rarely be applicable in respect of RRO matters and is limited in its application because it excludes appeals on a point of law – that is because such appeals are permitted by s.11 of the Tribunals, Courts and Enforcement Act 2007, as just discussed.

Other matters

Orders for costs

A significant difference exists between the Courts and the FTT – and also the Upper Tribunal – when it comes to the question of who, if anyone, should pay another party's legal costs incurred in respect of the RRO proceedings, such as the costs of solicitors and barristers.

The starting point both in the FTT and the Upper Tribunal is that the costs of and incidental to the proceedings in each are in that tribunal's discretion (s.29 (1) of the Tribunals, Courts and Enforcement Act 2007).

However, because of rule 13 of the FTT's Procedural Rules a party to RRO proceedings in the FTT – and the same point is applicable to the Upper Tribunal – is very rarely going to be ordered to pay the legal costs of another. The FTT when dealing with RROs is with rare exceptions likely to be a 'no costs arena', although see below in relation to tribunal fees that have been paid.

For the purposes of RROs and the HPA 2016, the relevant exceptions relate to the FTT's power to (a) award wasted costs along with the costs of applying for a wasted costs order and (b) to award costs where a party has acted unreasonably in bringing, defending or conducting proceedings (rule 13 of FTT's Procedural Rules).

The FTT may – not must – make an order for costs and even then only in limited circumstances expressly included in rule 13 of the FTT's Procedural Rules, which include the two just mentioned.

The first of these – "wasted costs" – relates to payment of legal costs incurred by a party *by* a legal or other representative where such costs are incurred:

> *"(a) as a result of any improper, unreasonable or negligent act or omission on the part of any legal or other representative or any employee of such a representative, or*
>
> *(b) which, in the light of any such act or omission occurring after they were incurred, the relevant Tribunal considers it is unreasonable to expect that party to pay."* (s. 29 (5) of the Tribunals, Courts and Enforcement Act 2007)

The reference to *"legal or other representative"* means any person exercising a right of audience or right to conduct the proceedings on his behalf (s. 29 (6) of the Tribunals, Courts and Enforcement Act 2007).

Secondly, the FTT may make an order in respect of costs if a person has acted unreasonably in bringing, defending or conducting proceedings (rule 13 (1) (b) of the FTT's Procedural Rules).

This threshold is a high one and is certainly not met simply because an application for an RRO or a defence to it has been rejected by the FTT. In *Willow Court Management Company (1985) Ltd v Alexander* [2016] UKUT 290 (LC) the Upper Tribunal by way of a 3-stage test gave guidance on how applications for costs based on this rule should be approached:

1) applying an objective standard of conduct to the facts of the case, has the person acted unreasonably? Unreasonable conduct of the person is key. It was said in that case that if there is no reasonable explanation for the conduct complained of, the behaviour will properly be adjudged to be unreasonable, and the threshold for the making of an order will have been crossed;

2) If the above is satisfied the FTT should then consider whether, in the light of the unreasonable conduct it has found to have been demonstrated, it ought to make an order for costs or not. This is a matter for the discretion of the FTT;

3) If the FTT finds that it ought to make an order for costs following this second step it is then a question of what the terms of that order should be.

As to step one – whether or not a person's behaviour is unreasonable – the Upper Tribunal in *Willow Court* said that although it was an objective fact if it was or not, it was a value judgment on which views might differ and that the standard of behaviour expected ought not to be set at an unrealistic level. 'Unreasonable' conduct was said to include conduct which was vexatious and designed to harass the other side, but it will not be enough that the conduct leads to an unsuccessful outcome. The 'acid test' was said to be whether or not there is a reasonable explanation for the conduct complained of.

In *Lea v. GP Ilfracombe Management Company Limite*d [2024] EWCA Civ 1241 the Court of Appeal declined to give general guidelines as to what may or may not amount to 'unreasonable conduct', following the approach in *Willow Court* that (i) deciding whether or not there has been unreasonable conduct and, if so, (ii) whether an adverse order for costs should be made is a fact-specific exercise. The Court further held that vexatious or harassing behaviour may be part of unreasonable conduct, but that it is not necessary for it to be.

Therefore, such costs' orders will rarely be made.

An example – but no more than that – of when costs relating to RRO proceedings have been ordered by the FTT to be paid by a party can be found in its decision in *Leibel v. Baird* CHI/29UC/HMF/2020/0035. As a decision of the FTT it has no binding authority (no other tribunal would have to follow it) but is interesting nevertheless as it relates to RRO proceedings.

An application for an RRO had been made to the FTT against a landlord by one tenant of five. The alleged offence said to have been committed by the landlord so as to entitle the tenant to the RRO was the offence of being in control of or managing an unlicensed HMO (s. 72 (1) of the Housing Act 2004). The landlord, however, defended by saying that there had been only four, not five, tenants – thereby, it was initially argued by the landlord, avoiding the HMO licensing requirements. The landlord produced a tenancy agreement naming only four tenants; the applicant tenant said that the version produced by the landlord was a forgery. The second day of the hearing, however, did not take place until around four weeks after the first day, at which point the landlord having obtained representation and having been ordered to disclose bank statements (showing payments from five people) admitted that the property had in fact required an HMO licence and therefore admitted that the offence had been committed, despite the initial defence.

As to the tenant's application against the landlord for costs to be paid to her pursuant to rule 13 (1) (b) of the FTT's Procedural Rules – a person having acted unreasonably in bringing, defending or conducting the proceedings – the FTT found that the landlord had in signing a statement of truth on the defence deliberately misled it. As for the version of the tenancy that was initially relied upon the by landlord:

> "[the landlord] *has deliberately produced a document which, placing it in the most generous light for* [them], is *not the document signed at that meeting and which the tenants believed was the tenancy agreement they were entering into. The production of this document was a calculated decision by* [the landlord] *in an attempt to mislead the Tribunal."*

In addition to an RRO in the sum of £5382 plus £300 for reimbursement of tribunal fees, the FTT ordered the landlord to pay the applicant tenant £21,512 for their solicitor costs and fees of their barrister.

Applications for costs may be made orally at a hearing or in writing but must be made within 28 days after the date on which the FTT sends its notice recording the decision which finally disposes of all issues in the proceedings or notice of consent to a withdrawal under rule 22 of the FTT's Procedural Rules ending the proceedings (rule 13 (5) of the FTT's Procedural Rules).

The FTT must give the party against whom the application for costs is made an opportunity to make representations, and it may summarily assess those costs or order that they be the subject of detailed assessment if not agreed. As a result of this the FTT also has a power to order an amount to be paid on account before the costs or expenses are assessed (rule 13 (6) to (9) of the FTT's Procedural Rules).

The position is the same for the Upper Tribunal. In this respect see rule 10 of the Upper Tribunal's Procedural Rules.

The FTT may also order a party to reimburse the fees that another has paid (see rule 13 (2) of the FTT's Procedural Rules).

Settlement and withdrawal of applications for RROs

The FTT's Procedural Rules allow for applications to be withdrawn (rule 22) and for the making of consent orders disposing of the proceedings (rule 35). Such procedures may, for example, be followed after an agreement to settle the RRO application has been reached. In this context, parties may seek to agree an amount to be paid in circumstances where it is clear that an offence has been committed and – assuming that the application is correct in all other respects – the only substantive dispute is going to relate to how much the order should be.

Proposed changes contained in the Renters' Rights Bill 2024-25

The Renters' Rights Bill 2024-25 is, at the time of writing, going through Parliament. As such the precise nature of the changes it is likely to make to the RRO regime in the HPA 2016 are currently unclear but that changes will be made and, generally speaking, that they will be in the form as contained in the Bill (or similar to) is highly likely.

Extension of time limits in respect of applications by tenants and LHAs

It is proposed that the 12-month limit currently in s. 41 (2) (b) of the HPA 2016 be extended to 24 months. In other words, the proposal would mean that a tenant could apply for an RRO if the offence was committed in the period of two years ending with the day on which the application is made (this being in addition to the requirement in s. 41 (2) (a) that the offence relate to housing that, at the time of the offence, was let to the tenant).

The time limit relating to applications by LHAs is also likely to be amended by changing s. 42 (5) (this is the provision relating to an LHA's duty to first serve on the landlord a notice of intended proceedings). Currently such a notice may not be given to the landlord by an LHA after the end of the period of 12 months beginning with the day on which the landlord committed the offence to which the notice relates. In line with applications made by tenants, the proposed change would increase this period to two years.

Summary

- Applications seeking an RRO are to be made to the FTT. Once satisfied that a proper application has been made and fee paid, it will usually direct the proceedings to a final hearing, after which a written decision with its reasons will be sent out to the parties;

- There is an important 12-month time limit relating to when applications can be brought (see s. 41 (2) (b) of the HPA 2016) in that a tenant can only apply for an RRO if the offence relied upon was committed in the period of 12 months ending with the day on which the application to the FTT is made;

- If an LHA is wanting to apply for an RRO against a landlord in relation to universal credit then it must first give the landlord a notice informing them of, amongst other matters, its intention to apply for the RRO. This is a pre-condition to be followed by LHAs before applying for an RRO, and like the above point the notice cannot be given after the end of the period of 12 months beginning with the day on which the landlord committed the offence that the LHA is relying upon;

- Both time limits are, however, to be extended by the Renters' Rights Bill to two years;

- The making or amount of an RRO by the FTT may in certain circumstances be challenged, usually where the FTT has made an error on a point of law;

- Such an appeal – to the Upper Tribunal – first requires the permission either of the FTT or the Upper Tribunal itself;

- In the vast majority of cases relating to RROs the FTT and the Upper Tribunal will not order the losing party to pay the winner's costs.

MORE BOOKS BY LAW BRIEF PUBLISHING

A selection of our other titles available now:-

'A Practical Guide to Probation Breaches and Other Applications' by Mark Thomas
'A Practical Guide to Remarriage and Divorce' by Cordelia Williams & Claire Howard
'A Practical Guide to Privacy, Transparency, Reporting Restrictions and Closed Proceedings in the Court of Protection' by Laura Mannering
'Beaumont on Barristers – A Guide to Defending Disciplinary Proceedings (Second Edition)' by Marc Beaumont
'A Practical Guide to Payments for Environmental Services' by Ben Sharples
'A Practical Guide to the Law of Pregnancy and Maternity at Work' by Rebecca Thomas
'A Practical Guide to Redundancy – Second Edition' by Philip Hyland & Collette Moore
'A Practical Guide to International Issues for Scottish Family Lawyers' by Susie Mountain, Donna McKay, Ken MacDonald
'A Practical Guide to the Law on Deprivation of Liberty' by Ben Troke
'A Practical Guide to Rights over Airspace and Subsoil – Second Edition' by Daniel Gatty
'A Practical Guide to the Law in Relation to Inquests' by Ramya Nagesh
'A Practical Guide to the Construction and Rectification of Wills and Trust Instruments (Second Edition)' by Edward Hewitt
'A Practical Guide to Data Protection in Social Housing' by Clare Paterson
'A Practical Guide to Spousal Maintenance – Second Edition' by Liz Cowell
'A Practical Guide to International Parental Child Abduction Law (England and Wales)' by Dr Onyója Momoh
'A Practical Guide to Deprivation of British Citizenship' by Sean Ell
'A Practical Guide to Commercial Property Service Charges' by Rachel Garton
'A Practical Guide to Clinical Negligence – Third Edition' by Geoffrey Simpson-Scott (Geoff)
'A Practical Guide to the Rights of Grandparents in Children Proceedings – Second Edition' by Stuart Barlow

'The Electronic Communications Code: A Practical Guide – Second Edition' by Kerry Bretherton KC, James Castle, Mark Loveday
'A Practical Guide to the Independent School Standards – September 2023 Edition' by Sarah McKimm
'A Practical Guide to Estate Administration and Crypto Assets' by Richard Marshall
'A Practical Guide to Parental Alienation in Private and Public Law Children Cases' by Sam King QC & Frankie Shama
'Contested Heritage – Removing Art from Land and Historic Buildings' by Richard Harwood QC, Catherine Dobson, David Sawtell
'The Limits of Separate Legal Personality: When Those Running a Company Can Be Held Personally Liable for Losses Caused to Third Parties Outside of the Company' by Dr Mike Wilkinson
'A Practical Guide to Transgender Law' by Robin Moira White & Nicola Newbegin
'A Practical Guide to 'Stranded Spouses' in Family Law' by Mani Singh Basi
'A Practical Guide to Residential Freehold Conveyancing' by Lorraine Richardson
'A Practical Guide to Pensions on Divorce for Lawyers' by Bryan Scant
'A Practical Guide to Challenging Sham Marriage Allegations in Immigration Law' by Priya Solanki
'A Practical Guide to Digital Communications Evidence in Criminal Law' by Sam Willis
'A Practical Guide to Legal Rights in Scotland' by Sarah-Jane Macdonald
'A Practical Guide to New Build Conveyancing' by Paul Sams & Rebecca East
'A Practical Guide to Inherited Wealth on Divorce' by Hayley Trim
'A Practical Guide to Practice Direction 12J and Domestic Abuse in Private Law Children Proceedings' by Rebecca Cross & Malvika Jaganmohan
'A Practical Guide to Confiscation and Restraint' by Narita Bahra QC, John Carl Townsend, David Winch
'A Practical Guide to the Law of Forests in Scotland' by Philip Buchan
'A Practical Guide to Health and Medical Cases in Immigration Law' by Rebecca Chapman & Miranda Butler
'A Practical Guide to Bad Character Evidence for Criminal Practitioners by Aparna Rao
'A Practical Guide to Extradition Law post-Brexit' by Myles Grandison et al
'A Practical Guide to Hoarding and Mental Health for Housing Lawyers' by Rachel Coyle

'Stephens on Contractual Indemnities' by Richard Stephens
'A Practical Guide to the EU Succession Regulation' by Richard Frimston
'A Practical Guide to Solicitor and Client Costs – Second Edition' by Robin Dunne
'Constructive Dismissal – Practice Pointers and Principles' by Benjimin Burgher
'A Practical Guide to Religion and Belief Discrimination Claims in the Workplace' by Kashif Ali
'A Practical Guide to the Law of Medical Treatment Decisions' by Ben Troke
'Fundamental Dishonesty and QOCS in Personal Injury Proceedings: Law and Practice' by Jake Rowley
'A Practical Guide to the Law in Relation to School Exclusions' by Charlotte Hadfield & Alice de Coverley
'A Practical Guide to Divorce for the Silver Separators' by Karin Walker
'The Right to be Forgotten – The Law and Practical Issues' by Melissa Stock
'A Practical Guide to Planning Law and Rights of Way in National Parks, the Broads and AONBs' by James Maurici QC, James Neill et al
'A Practical Guide to Election Law' by Tom Tabori
'A Practical Guide to the Law in Relation to Surrogacy' by Andrew Powell
'A Practical Guide to Claims Arising from Fatal Accidents – Second Edition' by James Patience
'A Practical Guide to Asbestos Claims' by Jonathan Owen & Gareth McAloon
'A Practical Guide to Stamp Duty Land Tax in England and Northern Ireland' by Suzanne O'Hara
'A Practical Guide to the Law of Farming Partnerships' by Philip Whitcomb
'A Practical Guide to the Law of Unlawful Eviction and Harassment – Second Edition' by Stephanie Lovegrove
'A Practical Guide to Costs in Personal Injury Claims – Second Edition' by Matthew Hoe
'A Practical Guide to the General Data Protection Regulation (GDPR) – Second Edition' by Keith Markham
'A Practical Guide to Working with Litigants in Person and McKenzie Friends in Family Cases' by Stuart Barlow
'Protecting Unregistered Brands: A Practical Guide to the Law of Passing Off' by Lorna Brazell
'A Practical Guide to Secondary Liability and Joint Enterprise Post-Jogee' by Joanne Cecil & James Mehigan

'A Practical Guide to the Pre-Action RTA Claims Protocol for Personal Injury Lawyers' by Antonia Ford

'A Practical Guide to Neighbour Disputes and the Law' by Alexander Walsh

'A Practical Guide to Coercive Control for Legal Practitioners and Victims' by Rachel Horman

'A Practical Guide to the Law of Driverless Cars – Second Edition'

by Alex Glassbrook, Emma Northey & Scarlett Milligan

'A Practical Guide to TOLATA Claims' by Greg Williams

'A Practical Guide to Elderly Law – Second Edition' by Justin Patten

'A Practical Guide to Responding to Housing Disrepair and Unfitness Claims' by Iain Wightwick

'A Practical Guide to the Law of Bullying and Harassment in the Workplace' by Philip Hyland

'How to Be a Freelance Solicitor: A Practical Guide to the SRA-Regulated Freelance Solicitor Model' by Paul Bennett

'A Practical Guide to Prison Injury Claims' by Malcolm Johnson

'A Practical Guide to Advising Clients at the Police Station' by Colin Stephen McKeown-Beaumont

'A Practical Guide to Antisocial Behaviour Injunctions – Second Edition' by Iain Wightwick

'Practical Mediation: A Guide for Mediators, Advocates, Advisers, Lawyers, and Students in Civil, Commercial, Business, Property, Workplace, and Employment Cases' by Jonathan Dingle with John Sephton

'The Mini-Pupillage Workbook' by David Boyle

'A Practical Guide to Crofting Law' by Brian Inkster

'A Practical Guide to the Law of Domain Names and Cybersquatting' by Andrew Clemson

'A Practical Guide to the Law of Gender Pay Gap Reporting' by Harini Iyengar

'NHS Whistleblowing and the Law' by Joseph England

'Employment Law and the Gig Economy' by Nigel Mackay & Annie Powell

'A Practical Guide to Noise Induced Hearing Loss (NIHL) Claims' by Andrew Mckie, Ian Skeate, Gareth McAloon

'An Introduction to Beauty Negligence Claims – A Practical Guide for the Personal Injury Practitioner' by Greg Almond

'Intercompany Agreements for Transfer Pricing Compliance' by Paul Sutton

'Zen and the Art of Mediation' by Martin Plowman

'A Practical Guide to Adoption for Family Lawyers' by Graham Pegg

'A Practical Guide to Industrial Disease Claims' by Andrew Mckie & Ian Skeate
'A Practical Guide to Conducting a Sheriff Court Proof' by Andrew Stevenson
'A Practical Guide to Vicarious Liability' by Mariel Irvine
'A Practical Guide to Applications for Landlord's Consent and Variation of Leases' by Mark Shelton
'A Practical Guide to Relief from Sanctions Post-Mitchell and Denton' by Peter Causton
'A Practical Guide to Equity Release for Advisors' by Paul Sams
'A Practical Guide to Financial Services Claims' by Chris Hegarty
'A Practical Guide to Financial Ombudsman Service Claims' by Adam Temple & Robert Scrivenor
'A Practical Guide to Running Housing Disrepair and Cavity Wall Claims – Second Edition' by Andrew Mckie & Ian Skeate
'A Practical Guide to Holiday Sickness Claims – Second Edition' by Andrew Mckie & Ian Skeate
'Arguments and Tactics for Personal Injury and Clinical Negligence Claims' by Dorian Williams
'A Practical Guide to Drone Law' by Rufus Ballaster, Andrew Firman, Eleanor Clot
'On Experts: CPR35 for Lawyers and Experts' by David Boyle
'An Introduction to Personal Injury Law' by David Boyle

These books and more are available to order online direct from the publisher at www.lawbriefpublishing.com, where you can also read free sample chapters. For any queries, call us on 0844 587 2383 or email us at mail@lawbriefpublishing.com.

Our books are all generally in stock at www.amazon.co.uk with free next day delivery for Prime members, and at good legal bookshops such as Wildy & Sons.

We are regularly launching new books in our series of practical day-to-day practitioners' guides. Visit our website and join our free newsletter to be kept informed and to receive special offers, free chapters, etc.

You can also follow us on Twitter at www.twitter.com/lawbriefpub.

www.ingramcontent.com/pod-product-compliance
Lightning Source LLC
LaVergne TN
LVHW022107200926
848481LV00003B/1084
* 9 7 8 1 9 1 6 6 9 8 7 0 3 *